| DATE | | |
|---|---|---|
| | | |
| | | |
| | | |
| | | |
| | | |
| | | |
| | | |
| | | |
| | | |
| | | |
| | | |
| | | |
| | | |

® THE BAKER & TAYLOR CO.

# FAULKNER'S HEROIC DESIGN

LYNN GARTRELL LEVINS

# FAULKNER'S HEROIC DESIGN

The Yoknapatawpha Novels

THE UNIVERSITY OF GEORGIA PRESS
ATHENS

Library of Congress Catalog Card Number: 74–18585
International Standard Book Number: 0–8203–0374–7
The University of Georgia Press, Athens 30602
© 1976 by the University of Georgia Press
Printed in the United States of America

Part of chapter 2 appeared as "The Four Narrative Perspectives in *Absalom, Absalom!,*" *PMLA*, 85 (January 1970), 35–47. I wish to express my appreciation to the editor of that publication for his kind permission to reprint it here.

TO MY PARENTS—

*Helen Bell and William Andrew Levins*

—IN GRATITUDE

# Contents

# Preface

Edith Hamilton once called Faulkner to task because his fiction was not heroic enough. She saw in him the supreme contemporary artist of the currently popular world of the absurd. This study is, in part, an answer to Miss Hamilton's accusation. In the pages which follow I have explored what I have called Faulkner's heroic design—his juxtaposition of the events of his rural community of Yoknapatawpha against scenes from and echoes of myths, classical drama, epic poetry, chivalric and historical romance. I have also explored the implications of this design—that Faulkner is affirming the existence of some principle of historical continuity which ties our era with a past that presupposes the significance of man and is asserting his belief that in the twentieth century the heroic is still possible.

This volume treats all the major Yoknapatawpha novels from *Sartoris* to *The Reivers.* I have chosen to organize the chapters not by individual work, however, but by mode. In this way I hope to show more clearly how Faulkner is using these heroic materials throughout the whole of the Yoknapatawpha canon.

It is my pleasant task to acknowledge the invaluable assistance of certain individuals. I wish to express my appreciation to Professors Weldon Thornton and Joseph M. Flora, who read the book in manuscript and who offered suggestions highly perceptive and gratefully received. To Professor C. Hugh Holman, who also read the manuscript and who gave freely of his advice, his own vast knowledge of Faulkner —and his encouragement, I owe an especial debt of thanks.

Finally I wish to acknowledge the publishers of Faulkner's works quoted in this study. All the editions are published at New York by Random House unless otherwise noted. *Absalom, Absalom!* (Modern Library, 1951); *A Fable* (Modern Library, 1966); *Go Down, Moses* (Modern Library, 1942); *The Hamlet* (1940); *Intruder in the Dust* (Modern Library, 1948); *Light in August* (Modern Library, 1950); *The Mansion* (1959); *Pylon* (New York: Harrison Smith and Robert Haas, 1935); *The Reivers* (1962); *Requiem for a Nun* (1951); *Sanctuary* (Modern Library, 1931); *Sartoris* (New York: Harcourt, Brace, 1929); *The Sound and the Fury* and *As I Lay Dying* (Modern Library, 1946); *The Town* (Vintage Books, 1957); *The Unvanquished* (1938); *The Wild Palms* (1939).

Lynn Gartrell Levins

# FAULKNER'S HEROIC DESIGN

## CHAPTER I

# Faulkner and the Mythical Method

In one of his class conferences at Charlottesville William Faulkner was asked about the origin of the title of *Light in August.* He replied that it referred to a particular glow in the air, that in Mississippi there are a few days in the middle of this summer month when the light has in it a luminous quality "of an older light than ours"—"as though it came not from just today but from back in the old classic times: It might," he said, "have fauns and satyrs and the gods— from Greece, from Olympus in it somewhere."[1] Lena Grove, Faulkner's marvelous creation who manages to cope with every crisis that confronts her simply because she does not even know that she is being tried, also possesses this same "pagan quality," Faulkner goes on to say—the kind of a woman who had as little concern for the conventional laws of the time as "the women . . . on whom Jupiter begot children were anxious for a home and a father." This juxtaposition of the contemporary scene with an older time than ours is the same literary technique which Eliot saw and appreciated in Joyce's *Ulysses* and which he termed the "mythical method"—the manipulation of a "continuous parallel between contemporaneity and antiquity."[2] In commenting on his novel's title, Faulkner, once having drawn attention to this idea of a parallel, then, as was so often his wont, appeared to pass it off lightly. "It was just to me a pleasant evocative title," he said, "because it reminded me of that time, of a luminosity older than our Christian civilization." Nevertheless scenes from and echoes of myths, classical drama, epic poetry, chivalric and historical romance—all of which serve to remind the reader of an older time than ours—appear in the Yoknapatawpha canon with such frequency and in such prominence that they bear examination.

In *As I Lay Dying* the obstacles which the members of the Bundren family encounter in their efforts to bury Addie are the same obstacles which confronted the old epic heroes—the ancient catastrophes of flood and fire. The very nature of the Bundren pilgrimage—an odyssey to bury the wife and mother in her family cemetery at Jefferson—evokes the voyage to the land of the dead undertaken by Odysseus, Aeneas, and Dante. By means of these allusions Faulkner intends for the funeral procession from Frenchman's Bend to Jefferson to be viewed as an epic journey. The episode of Ike and the cow in *The Hamlet* suggests in both event and tone the medieval romance. By defending the object of his love—called at once Astarte, Juno, Troy's Helen— from water, fire, and "dragon," Ike Snopes is to be seen as a modern-day protagonist of the knightly tales of valor. Although the tone is by no means romantic, still the subject matter of *Old Man* is essentially chivalric, and the tall convict and the woman in the tree become the counterpoint not only to Harry and Charlotte in *The Wild Palms,* but also to the couple in medieval literature who sacrificed all for love. If Faulkner's presentation of his knight-errant is largely comic, the humor does not negate the trials which his protagonist undergoes and overcomes for the sake of a woman he does not even know.[3] The tall convict withstands whatever is thrust at him—the great flood, the sojourn on the snake-infested island, the onslaught first by the gang of criminals and again by the band of soldiers—and all for the most praiseworthy of motives: to do his duty for the sake of "his good name, his responsibility not only toward those who were responsible toward him but to himself, his own honor in the doing of what was asked of him, his pride in being able to do it, no matter what it was" (*The Wild Palms*, p. 166). The point is that Faulkner, in each case, is not parodying traditional literary modes by focusing on the grotesque diminution of legend and myth in Yoknapatawpha County; but rather he is writing in *As I Lay Dying* and *Old Man* and *The Hamlet* of the fulfillment of an ethical obligation, and when the obligation is accomplished in spite of temptations to abandon it and difficulties to thwart it, then the action of Anse Bundren or the tall convict or the idiot Ike Snopes approaches heroic proportions.

By placing the events in Yoknapatawpha in a framework of mythic and literary allusion Faulkner is enlarging their meaning. He is similarly elevating the inhabitants of his imaginary region by identifying them with forces greater than themselves. In *Absalom, Absalom!*, for example, Faulkner is concerned with the re-creation of history, as each of his four fictional narrators accepts certain facts and discards others in an effort to endow the Sutpen story with motive and meaning. For three of the narrators the members of the House of Sutpen are figures larger than life: for Rosa Coldfield, Thomas Sutpen is the Gothic villain "out of a tale to frighten children with"; to Mr. Compson he is the Greek hero contending against Fate, his environment, and his fellow man; and to Quentin he is simply a minor character in a chivalric drama, whose participants are his children Charles, Judith, and Henry. Faulkner himself conceived of the Sutpen story as Mr. Compson did, as a drama possessing the simple heroic attributes of the characters in ancient Greek literature. Years later at the University of Virginia Faulkner revealed that he saw Sutpen as the old Greek hero—a man who "wanted a son . . . and he got too many sons—his sons destroyed one another and then him" (*Faulkner in the University,* p. 35). The thematic pattern of the novel itself bears out this tragic design of *Absalom, Absalom!:* the analogies between Sutpen and Oedipus, Sutpen's sons and Eteocles and Polyneices, Judith and Antigone; the presence of a curse which is passed on from Thomas Sutpen to each succeeding generation and which makes the Sutpen dynasty a contemporary House of Atreus; the choice of Clytemnestra as a name for Sutpen's Negro daughter; the scene describing the burning of Sutpen's Hundred which is to be compared, in event and tone, to a similar scene in Euripides' *Orestes.*

By setting the actions of his Yoknapatawpha characters within the framework of Greek tragedy, or chivalric romance, or the epic, Faulkner adds to his fictional locale a mythical dimension, which is to be distinguished from, say, the John Sartoris myth, or the making of a wildly extravagant romanticism. Behind the chivalric framework of the tall convict's actions, behind the Bundren pilgrimage as epic journey or the identification of Thomas Sutpen as the old Greek tragic hero lies the concept of the existence of a heroic ideal, which for Faulkner is representative of what people are capable of—both the baseness and the grandeur.[4] The episode in *The Sound and the Fury* of Quentin and Caddy in Hell is an echo of the *Divine Comedy.* When he desires an eternal union with Caddy in the "clean flame" of Hell, Quentin makes it known that he is willing to join the score of chivalric lovers before him who have been sentenced to Purgatory for the service they performed for love. The scene in *The Hamlet* in which Flem challenges Satan and wins is evocative of both the *Inferno* and the

[4]

Faust legend. The humor in the episode cannot be denied, yet what is significant here is that never again can the reader see Flem as simply an aggrandizing hill farmer, for somehow cosmic forces have entered in. In the same novel there is a similar transformation of Eula Varner Snopes. Wearing the flowing nightgown and with her hair in one long braid, Eula, after her marriage to Flem, is no longer a source for humor, but she becomes a Valkyrie, a figure worthy now of tragedy.

In the pages which follow I attempt to examine what I have called the heroic design of Yoknapatawpha. I also attempt to explore the implications of that design—not the least of which may provide a possible answer to those who see a contradiction between Faulkner's optimistic public statements about his fiction and a darker voice expressed in the fiction itself. In his introduction to *William Faulkner: Three Decades of Criticism,* in which he summarizes critical commentary on Faulkner up to 1960, Frederick J. Hoffman succinctly focuses on the dilemma: "The wonder grew," he states, "that this man who had described so powerfully and so frequently the ugly, chaotic, miserable, obscene, irrational world of man should have meant all along that he was upholding the eternal verities and therefore had been without qualification on the side of the angels."[5] Faulkner's world of Yoknapatawpha, as it is described by Hoffman, is the currently popular world of the absurd. It could find no better fictional mouthpiece in Faulkner than his classic example of the cynical nihilist, the alcoholic patriarch of the Compson family. Man is the "stalemate of dust and desire," Mr. Compson tells Quentin; and "victory is an illusion of philosophers and fools" (*The Sound and the Fury,* pp. 143, 95).

But there is often a danger in searching through a writer's fiction in an effort to find a spokesman for that writer, and never more so than with Faulkner. In "Delta Autumn" the eighty-year-old Isaac McCaslin returns once again to the woods which give him peace. Sitting by the campsite he answers his young kinsman, Roth Edmonds, who, in his disparagement of the human condition, has more than a little in common with Quentin's father. "There are good men everywhere, at all times," Ike says. "Most men are. Some are just unlucky, because most men are a little better than their circumstances give them a chance to be" (*Go Down, Moses*, p. 345). Isaac McCaslin's refutation of Roth's attitude is supported by the mythic and literary allusions which run throughout the Yoknapatawpha canon. These allusions constitute a heroic framework which opposes the idea that modern man is insignificant because he is cut off from anything greater than himself; and instead they imply some principle of historical continuity which ties our era with the golden age of antiquity. In *The Mansion* once Mink Snopes kills his cousin Flem and thereby accomplishes his quest, he becomes one with the old heroes of legend and myth: "Equal to any, good as any, brave as any, being inextricable from, anonymous with all of them: the beautiful, the splendid, the proud and the brave, right on up to the very top itself . . . Helen and the bishops, the kings and the unhomed angels, the scornful and graceless seraphim" (pp. 435–36). For Faulkner in the twentieth century the heroic is still possible, where "most men," as Isaac McCaslin says, "are a little better than their circumstances give them a chance to be."

[6]

# CHAPTER II

# The Heroic Design

*Absalom, Absalom!* tells the story of Thomas Sutpen as that
story is reconstructed by four fictional narrators who interpret and try to order the palpable world of experience from
four different points of view. In one sense the novel can be
seen as an attempt to dramatize the process through which
historical "truth" is re-created. Faulkner himself indicated
that he fully intended the story of Thomas Sutpen's thirty-
six-year invasion of Yoknapatawpha County to be considered as a part of southern history. By including at the end
of the novel the chronological list of biographical information, the author makes it evident that the Sutpen story did
"happen," that the events of his life have behind them the
firm foundation of fact. In the four narrators' attempts to
reconstruct the past there are certain data available that are
regarded as valid—the dates of Sutpen's marriage and death,
the murder of Charles Bon by Henry Sutpen. However there
are also the all-important and as-yet-undiscovered motives
for the deeds done—why Bon was killed, why Rosa Coldfield "died" in 1865. To the four fictional storytellers a right
reading of certain events, such as the shot at the gate and
Wash Jones's murder of Sutpen, will uncover the whole
meaning of the story. But because neither Rosa, Mr. Compson, Quentin, nor Shreve were present at these crucial moments, their reconstruction of history is largely an interpre-
tive act of the imagination. And because three of the

[7]

narrators are emotionally involved in the southerner's shared past, they exaggerate fact into myth and transform history into legend.

In *Absalom, Absalom!* the Sutpen legend is pieced together, like so many parts to a jigsaw puzzle, by the four narrators. Rosa Coldfield, Mr. Compson, Quentin Compson, and Shreve McCannon, in creating their individual visions of Thomas Sutpen, combine objectively observed facts with imaginative speculation in an effort to endow certain events of the past with motive and meaning. The "facts" of the Sutpen story, assumed to be valid, are, as Mr. Compson tells Quentin, "just incredible"; alone "they dont explain":

Yes, Judith, Bon, Henry, Sutpen: all of them. They are there, yet something is missing; they are like a chemical formula exhumed along with the letters from that forgotten chest, carefully, the paper old and faded and falling to pieces, the writing faded, almost indecipherable, yet meaningful, familiar in shape and sense . . . you bring them together in the proportions called for, but nothing happens; you re-read, tedious and intent, poring, making sure that you have forgotten nothing, made no miscalculation; you bring them together again and again nothing happens: just the words, the symbols, the shapes themselves, shadowy inscrutable and serene, against that turgid background of a horrible and bloody mischancing of human affairs. (pp. 100–101)

Each narrator, in searching for the missing pieces that will allow him to read the faded writing, accepts certain facts, discards others, and fills the unexplained gap between action and motive with conjecture. Faulkner has carefully chosen his narrators so that each of the four fictional observers can weigh, judge, and interpret the Sutpen legend from a different perspective, determined by the observer's own particular generation and his personal relationship to the southern myth or to Colonel Sutpen, whose story becomes, to three

[8]

of the narrators, the microcosm of an entire region during a certain period in its history. Each narrator, by reacting to the fragmented pieces of the Sutpen puzzle with an individual response, creates his own version of "truth," and the result is that not one figure of Thomas Sutpen emerges by the end of the novel, but four.

In terms of pure narrative technique *Absalom, Absalom!* is a significant experiment in fiction. In both *The Sound and the Fury* and *As I Lay Dying* Faulkner differentiates those sections which present a different individual consciousness by means of deliberate variations in language and style. The distinction among the narratives in *Absalom,* however, does not involve variations of style, but form. Each viewpoint in the novel is shaped after a different literary genre: the Gothic, the Greek tragedy, the chivalric romance, and the tall tale. It is a skillful adaptation of form to meaning, for the four genres express, structurally, the particular emotional involvement of the fictional storyteller: Rosa Coldfield, haunted by the moral "outrage" inflicted by the "satanic" Sutpen, shapes her narrative to the Gothic mystery; Mr. Compson, doomed to believe in the grandeur of the South, relates his narrative as a Greek tragedy; Quentin, obsessed by Henry's relationship with Judith because of his own involvement with Caddy (presented in *The Sound and the Fury*) expresses his narrative in the framework of the chivalric romance; and Shreve, the detached northerner, convinced that the "unbelievable" South "is better than Ben Hur" (p. 217), relieves the intensity of the preceding viewpoints by means of the ludicrous humor of the tall tale. At the same time by choosing these particular literary modes, Faulkner intends for the reader to see the participants in the Sutpen legend as not merely human, but either as something more or something less than life-size. Moreover, by portraying Sutpen alternately as Gothic villain or

[9]

Greek hero or a figure in a chivalric drama, Faulkner has his protagonist operate against a grand scale of heroic action, which is to be distinguished, either by exceptional grandeur or baseness, from the ordinary world of everyday events.

Faulkner opens the tale at its highest pitch when he chooses to introduce the reader first to the figure of Thomas Sutpen as it is created by the imagination of Rosa Coldfield. Rosa presents her interpretation of the Sutpen story in the first chapter of the novel and again in the italicized fifth chapter, in which she provides a violent contrast to Mr. Compson's previous control, which is effected through irony. Both sections are narrated in Faulkner's most turgid, ponderous, and convoluted prose style. Throughout the two chapters, from beginning to end, there is no abatement of—and hence relief from—the acute intensity of the strained rhetoric.

It is Rosa Coldfield's personal tragedy that she must suffer the barren existence which is the result of an isolation of self from the necessary contact with concrete experience. "Living in that womb-like corridor where the world came not even as living echo but as dead incomprehensible shadow" (p. 162), Rosa is doomed to a secondhand "conception of the sun from seeing it through a piece of smoky glass" (p. 145). Because Rosa never saw nor heard the actual Charles Bon, but only glimpsed a photograph of him, he exists for her "in some shadow-realm of make-believe" (p. 147). Rosa has knowledge only of the imagination's world of illusion. When she does confront reality, she can comprehend it only in terms of the dreamer's limited knowledge of make-believe. Similarly, when reality threatens Rosa's peaceful world of illusion, as Thomas Sutpen did when he proposed a testing, before marriage, of Rosa's ability to give birth to a male heir, then that reality assumes a nightmarish quality, as it does when a sleeper is awakened from a deep sleep. In consequence Rosa both interprets the world around her and expresses herself to this world in light of the dreamer's separation from reality. Rosa's language, then, is the language of the dreamer, which with its hallucinatory tone possesses that heightened intensity which will pervade, in varying degrees, the entire reconstruction of the legend.

The setting in which Rosa tells Quentin about Sutpen's settlement in Yoknapatawpha County partakes of the stifling aura which surrounds the narrator—"a grim mausoleum air of Puritan righteousness and outraged female vindictiveness" (p. 60). The dim, hot, airless room, with blinds fastened and doors bolted, becomes a tomb where Rosa Coldfield retires to shut herself off from reality. Existing in this "coffin-smelling gloom," Rosa seems almost as much a ghost as the shadowy figures she evokes from the past. She herself admits that her life had been "destined to end on an afternoon in April forty-three years ago" (p. 18), when Thomas Sutpen insulted the Puritan values by means of which Rosa Coldfield had weighed and judged her world. Rosa, though a "ghost" for forty-three years, refuses to let the memory of the insult die. Believing that the only chance to give meaning, and thereby identity, to her life lies in her ability to avenge herself on an object dead for forty years, she is compelled to re-create for Quentin the owner of Sutpen's Hundred. The "outrage" which obsesses each waking moment of Rosa's life also haunts her "grim haggard amazed" voice, and gives it that "logic- and reason-flouting quality of a dream" (p. 22). The dead figures which this voice calls into being thus people a shadowy dreamlike world; and Thomas Sutpen, the object of Rosa Coldfield's indomitable frustration, becomes the demon of the nightmare, the phantom-villain of a Gothic thriller.

The first narrative of the Sutpen story serves to sketch

[11]

the bare outlines of Sutpen, Judith, Henry, and Bon, which will later be given shape and completed in detail by the remaining points of view. Because Rosa Coldfield immerses the created events in the unreality of a dream-vision, which is without logic and reason, Sutpen's actions are presented to the reader without explanation, and hence without the plausibility afforded by a cause-and-effect sequence. Thomas Sutpen's arrival in Mississippi possesses no firmer substance than a sudden materialization from out of thin air:

Out of quiet thunderclap he would abrupt (man-horse-demon) upon a scene peaceful and decorous as a schoolprize water color, faint sulphur-reek still in hair clothes and beard, with grouped behind him his band of wild niggers like beasts half tamed to walk upright like men, in attitudes wild and reposed, and manacled among them the French architect with his air grim, haggard, and tatter-ran. . . . Then in the long unamaze Quentin seemed to watch them overrun the hundred square miles of tranquil and astonished earth and drag house and formal gardens violently out of the soundless Nothing . . . creating the Sutpen's Hundred, the *Be Sutpen's Hundred* like the oldentime *Be Light.* (pp. 8–9)

Rosa is both unable and unwilling to acknowledge the object of her vengeance as being a mortal man, motivated by the same hopes and fears common to humanity. She endows his actions with larger-than-life proportions, interpreting each as being effected by Sutpen's strange supernatural powers. Thus Sutpen's Hundred is not a product of hard work by a band of wild Negroes and one French architect, but is a demonic edifice, conjured into being by three Satanic words. When Quentin tries to bring some control over Rosa Coldfield's distorted and nightmarish interpretation by stating that Sutpen simply *"built a plantation,"* that "grim haggard amazed" voice cries out, *"tore violently a plantation"* (p. 9).

Thomas Sutpen's arrival in Jefferson, his construction of Sutpen's Hundred, and his marriage to Ellen, as presented

by Rosa Coldfield, assume fantastically distorted proportions, because they are largely fabricated by the imagination
of a woman interested not in what actually happened, but
in what she wants to believe happened: "But even when I
saw [Sutpen's Hundred] for the first time that I could
remember I seemed already to know how it was going to
look just as I seemed to know how Ellen and Judith and
Henry would look before I saw them for the time which I
always remember as being the first" (p. 26). The most "demonic" action ascribed to Thomas Sutpen—the savage
gladiatorial combat between Sutpen and the wild Negro,
attended by the hysterical Henry and the fascinated Judith—is minutely described by a narrator who admits that
she was not even there. Rosa Coldfield does witness Sutpen's
wild carriage race to church, but the Puritan onlooker
refuses to see any humor in such a deed. It is interpreted
as Rosa interprets all Sutpen's actions—as an unnatural act
"logically" committed by a demon from Hell. Rosa's imagination thus re-creates, to Quentin, an "ogre or a djinn"
driving some otherworld chariot "in a thunder and a fury
of wildeyed horses and of galloping and of dust" (p. 23).

Rosa Coldfield's narration of the Sutpen story is, like the
conventional Gothic tale, centered around the doomed castle. Sutpen's Hundred is imagined by Rosa to be an earthly
Purgatory, a "grim ogre-bourne" (p. 167), which is sealed
off, "without a window or door or bedstead" (p. 16), from
the rest of humanity. The guardian of this Hell Gate is
Sutpen's Negro daughter Clytie, who, by virtue of being
fathered by "fell darkness" (p. 140), becomes the "cold
Cerberus of [Sutpen's] private hell" (p. 136). Like its Hades-
protected builder "who, being a demon," is therefore imper-
vious to the Civil War's "shot and shell" (p. 169), this
"indomitable skeleton," which the war's flames dare not
assail (p. 136), is "reserved for something more: some desola-

[13]

tion more profound than ruin" (p. 136). The strange and inexplicable noises that haunt the castles of the Gothic novel also haunt Sutpen's Hundred, and Rosa accordingly prefers to believe she hears "the house itself speaking again, though [in reality] it was Judith's voice" (p. 142). To Rosa Coldfield, who possesses the overly sensitive and disordered imagination that characterizes Anne Radcliffe's heroines, "the sabbath afternoon quiet of that house" sounds "louder than thunder, louder than laughing even with triumph" (p. 27).

Like the characters created by Matthew ("Monk") Lewis, the central figure of Rosa's Gothic tale of horror is suspected of an identification with the devil himself. Thomas Sutpen, "antedating time and house and doom and all" (p. 136), is "the beast out of a tale to frighten children with" (p. 158). This "ogre-djinn," this "light-blinded bat-like image," is not of this world, but is, instead, "cast by the fierce demoniac lantern up from beneath the earth's crust" (p. 171). Villain as well as demon (p. 169), Sutpen is the mysterious and gloomy tyrant of the tales of terror. In accordance with the Gothic tradition, he is, in Rosa's eyes, the perpetrator of horrible deeds against innocent victims. To sustain the identification of Thomas Sutpen with Satan, Sutpen's wife, Ellen Coldfield, is compared to Persephone. Like the mythological daughter of Ceres, Ellen is (in the mind of her sister Rosa) suddenly ravished by some ruling power of darkness and then allowed, by means of infrequent visits to church, "to return through a dispensation of one day only, to the world which she had quitted" (p. 23). Similarly, to Rosa, Henry and Judith, "the two half phantom children" (p. 167) conceived by "the demon in a kind of nightmare" (p. 13), are condemned either to an imprisonment in Sutpen's Hundred or to an early death (p. 139). This family, doomed by "their devil's heritage" (p. 135), is beset by the same malevolent destiny that hangs over the House of Manfred in Horace Walpole's *Castle of Otranto*, and that ends Manfred's lordship of Otranto by depriving him of any heirs. Thus the sole purpose of the Civil War—interpreted by the Puritan narrator to be a beneficial act of God—is to *"stay this demon and efface his name and lineage from the earth"* (p. 11).

Rosa Coldfield's narrative is immersed in the atmosphere of the mysterious unexplained terror that characterizes the Gothic novel. Events are divested of both cause and logical explanation, and are described in terms of their emotional effect on the fictional narrator. Thus Rosa repeats again and again that her experience on the "nightmare flight of stairs" (p. 149), following the murder of Charles Bon by Henry Sutpen, was a fearful one in which she, the dreamer, runs "without moving from a terror . . . you cannot believe, toward a safety in which you have no faith" (p. 142). The cause of the terror, the hidden darkness at the top of the stairs, remains unrevealed; and only the anticipation—the "profoundly attentive and distracted listening to or for something"—is described in order to heighten the suspense of the final revelation. To intensify the sense of the uncanny, the individuals Rosa Coldfield meets on the staircase are dispossessed of physical substance, and become only shadows and distorted parts. Thus, Rosa confronts, not Clytie's "familiar coffee-colored face" and body (p. 137), but "only the hand"—"the hand gone before [she] realized that it had been removed" (p. 142). Similarly the outraged Puritan encounters no identifiable human speaker but only the disembodied "sound of the other voice, the single word spoken from the stairhead above" (p. 139). This aura of suspense evoked by "the inexplicable unseen" (p. 138) reaches a climax at the end of Rosa Coldfield's narrative

[15]

with the unexplained, unfinished statement that there is something in Sutpen's Hundred—something "living hidden in that house" (p. 172).

The language in Rosa Coldfield's narrative is deliberately inflated and carried to an extreme. It is the outraged and agonized cry of a woman seduced in mind, if not in body, by the overwhelming power of Thomas Sutpen: "I saw that man return—the evil's source and head which had outlasted all its victims—who had created two children not only to destroy one another and his own line, but my line as well, yet I agreed to marry him" (p. 18). The emotionally compelling quality of this language, which mesmerizes the listening Quentin, is suited to the Gothic framework of Rosa's perspective. More than any other literary tradition the Gothic genre produces in the reader an affective response, by eliciting from him fear and terror through suspenseful anticipation. By a skillful manipulation of the dreamer's disregard for logic and an outraged woman's tendency to distort reality until it seems fantasy, Faulkner dramatically presents the skeletal outline of Thomas Sutpen divested of all reason and cause, and thereby he catches up the reader through a purposeful use of withheld information.

The control to Rosa Coldfield's hallucinatory depiction of Thomas Sutpen is Mr. Compson's perspective. Through the use of irony and through a rational approach to the piecing together of the puzzle, Quentin's father effects a detachment lacking in the preceding narrative. By means of this detachment Mr. Compson avoids that degree of distortion which results when the narrator is hopelessly involved with the figure he is trying to re-create, and he is thereby able to "humanize," through his perspective, Miss Rosa's shadowy phantom from Hell.

Although Thomas Sutpen's sudden arrival in Yok-

napatawpha County, without apparent reason or explanation, and with purpose and origin unknown, appears at first,
as in Rosa Coldfield's presentation, a creation "out of thin
air" (p. 32), there follows a detailed description of Sutpen's
physical characteristics which reveals this figure of "fell
darkness" to be of flesh and blood. Similarly his behavior,
which Rosa ascribed to an infernal nature, is explained in
terms of human motivation. Mr. Compson interprets the
building of Sutpen's Hundred and Henry Sutpen's feelings
toward Charles Bon as stemming from the eternal universal
verities, and from that special regional atmosphere which
envelops the southerner and shapes his way of thinking. It
is this sociological dimension—the relating of Thomas
Sutpen and his "design" to a particular culture and tradition—which Mr. Compson's perspective significantly adds
to Rosa Coldfield's point of view.

Although Mr. Compson, unlike Rosa Coldfield, has no
personal contact with Sutpen, he does possess the southerner's inherited veneration for those long-dead heroes who
deified themselves by fighting against General Sherman. To
Quentin's father not only is Thomas Sutpen such a man,
but his design is interpreted as a microcosm of the history
and heritage of the South. Because Sutpen's story becomes
"the complete statement of Southern ambition, execution
and success, guilt, doom, and destruction . . . as exemplified
by the action of one man,"[1] Mr. Compson, the doomed
southerner, is compelled like Rosa Coldfield to exaggerate
the figure central to his narration. But unlike Rosa's shade
the vision of Sutpen as imagined by Quentin's father is
without the demonic aura of a Satanic nature. On the contrary Thomas Sutpen as protagonist of Mr. Compson's narrative is the man of heroic stature who is celebrated in
southern myth. Through an elevation effected by exaggeration, the social situation assumes cosmic proportions and the

central participant becomes the Greek hero operating against a backdrop of fate and eternity.

Aristotle's definition of tragedy and the rules for its construction seem significantly applicable to Mr. Compson's narration of the Sutpen story. An integral feature of tragedy (as proposed in the *Poetics*), and one which distinguishes this literary mode from comedy and the epic, is its presentation in a dramatic rather than a narrative form. Similarly, in contrast to the other perspectives that employ the narrative method, Mr. Compson's viewpoint is expressed in language that suggests a drama being performed. The characters in this particular perspective are actors "entering upon the stage" to perform in a play—in "the pageant, the scene, the act" (p. 193). The setting—Sutpen's Hundred—and Judith's and her father's tombstones are the actors' props—"cleaned and polished and arranged by scene shifters who with the passing of twilight would return and strike them and carry them, hollow fragile and without weight, back to the warehouse until they should be needed again" (p. 193). Furthermore Mr. Compson makes it apparent that the drama being enacted is no insignificant contemporary production but is instead a classical tragedy. This stage manager, "striking the set and dragging on the synthetic and spurious shadows and shapes of the next one" is "Fate, destiny, retribution, irony . . . call him what you will" (pp. 72–73), Fate which plays as great a role in classical tragedy as any of the actors. Finally the costume for the actors is the simple "mask in Greek tragedy, interchangeable . . . from scene to scene . . . and behind which the events and occasions took place without chronology or sequence" (p. 62).

Aristotle says that the greatest tragedies, those most conducive to producing the tragic emotions of pity and fear, are the ones which involve the members of a particular house, so that the tragic deed is done within the family. Mr. Compson's version focuses on familial relationships by viewing the inhabitants of Sutpen's Hundred as members of a modern House of Atreus. Sutpen, the father, is the engenderer of an "ancient curse" (p. 204) that is passed on to each successive generation. Because of the curse Fate singles out the Sutpen family "in preference to any other in the county or the land" (p. 102) to receive the revenge meted out by the gods. As a consequence Henry Sutpen is doomed and destined to kill just as he is doomed to surrender and sacrifice. Similarly, in the third generation, Charles Etienne de Saint Velery Bon inherits, from Thomas Sutpen, "a furious and indomitable desperation," which he had acquired in his youth "from the walls in which the demon had lived, the air which he had once walked in and breathed until that moment when his own fate which he had dared in his turn struck back at him" (pp. 202–203). As it did against the House of Atreus, Fate decrees the Sutpen family—that "fecundity of dragon's teeth" (p. 62) sown by the perpetrator of the curse—to destroy one another. By means of the murder of Charles Bon, Henry is destined to play the "final part in his family's doom" (p. 86). This act ironically pronounces Jim Bond, the idiot youth who is part Negro, the sole survivor of the doomed line of Sutpen, the heir to the proposed dynasty.

Only in Mr. Compson's perspective does Thomas Sutpen approach the grand concept of the tragic hero—"a man not pre-eminently virtuous and just, whose misfortune, however, is brought upon him not by vice and depravity but by some error of judgment."[2] Miss Rosa's imagined vision of Sutpen is endowed with a certain magnitude, but it is that associated with the Satanic powers of a fantasy-created demon, motivated in everything he does by his viciously depraved nature. Shreve's lecherous "impotent old man" is a

[19]

ludicrous caricature of a human being, who not only lacks the stature of the Greek hero, but falls embarrassingly short of life-size proportions. In contrast the actors in Mr. Compson's drama possess the simple, heroic attributes of the characters in ancient Greek literature:

People too as we are, and victims too as we are, but victims of a different circumstance, simpler and therefore, integer for integer, larger, more heroic and the figures therefore more heroic too, not dwarfed and involved but distinct, uncomplex who had the gift of loving once or dying once instead of being diffused and scattered creatures drawn blindly limb from limb from a grab bag and assembled, author and victim too of a thousand homicides and a thousand copulations and divorcements. (p. 89)

Mr. Compson's Thomas Sutpen, the leading performer in the play, is, like the Greek hero, a man of great reputation and prosperity. Accordingly the citizens of Jefferson, chanting Thomas Sutpen's arrival in Yoknapatawpha County "in steady strophe and antistrophe: *Sutpen. Sutpen. Sutpen*" (p. 32), are the Greek chorus, announcing the entry of the protagonist onstage. Living "in the Spartan shell of the largest edifice in the county" (p. 39), Mr. Compson's created shade is the man who, *"given the occasion and the need. . . can and will do anything"*(p. 46). Like the Greek hero Sutpen dares to defy Circumstance—that particular state of affairs which sanctions one man's ordering another to go around to the back door. When he dares to defy these men who affirm they are superior because they own the plantations and the black men who maintain the plantations, then Sutpen, asserting the immortality and equality of Man, approaches the Promethean figure of Aeschylus' drama.

Sutpen, like the classical hero, is doomed to fall—a victim of the impersonal, hostile forces around him and of his own tragic flaw. To witness the inevitable doom, Clytie, no longer the Cerberean watchdog of a Satanic master, becomes, in Mr. Compson's section, the mythological Cassandra, "the presiding augur of [Sutpen's] disaster" (p. 62). Thomas Sutpen is also destined to failure in Rosa Coldfield's and Shreve McCannon's narratives, but here the failure ensues because of either a demonic nature or an impotence of strength and power. It is only in Mr. Compson's perspective that the error of judgment, as defined in Greek tragedy, is introduced. Mr. Compson's protagonist is aware that he is permitted but one mistake in his design (p. 53), and when it fails he continually asks himself at what one point did he misjudge his purpose. Sutpen's *hamartia* is the miscalculation he makes in his first marriage. This mistake ultimately leads to Sutpen's downfall because of the particular nature of his moral imperfection—an inability to repudiate the South's tradition once he knew that it was wrong. By renouncing the right of inheritance to any Negro heir, Sutpen—the Greek hero "not pre-eminently virtuous and just" —sacrifices to his now-immoral ambition his "pity and gentleness and love and all the soft virtues" (p. 154).

Because of his act of defiance Sutpen incurs the wrath of the gods. Mr. Compson reminds Quentin of the consequences of defying both the established tradition of an entire region and the unwritten laws of humanity; and he reveals that at the height of Sutpen's "role of arrogant ease and leisure," "Fate, destiny, retribution, irony . . . was already striking the set and dragging on the . . . shadows and shapes of the next one" (pp. 72–73). The next scene is the war's ruining of the once-Spartan ruler of the county. By juxtaposing two such scenes Mr. Compson includes in his narrative the peripety of Greek drama—a change from one state of things within the play to its opposite—specifically a change from happiness in the hero's fortunes to misery.

Because Mr. Compson's protagonist is elevated to heroic

proportions, Fate, the classic avenging force, requires no less a catastrophe than the Civil War to quell the titanic striving of its opponent—that "fateful mischance" laying waste the "black foundation" on which Sutpen's Hundred had been erected and "removing its two male mainstays, husband and son" (p. 78). Although Sutpen is doomed to failure in Rosa's, Mr. Compson's, and Shreve's narratives, it is only in Mr. Compson's section that he is ennobled after his fall because of the magnitude of what he has tried to do. "Weighing . . . circumstance against human nature, his own fallible judgment and mortal clay against not only human but natural forces" (p. 53), Thomas Sutpen—the Greek hero contending against his fellowman, his environment, and Fate itself—dares to attempt his design in defiance not only of society, but of eternity too. Because of the height of his fall and the courage in defiance against overwhelming odds, the Thomas Sutpen of Mr. Compson's perspective is able to arouse the pity absent in Rosa Coldfield's demon and the fear that Shreve's caricatured "hero" is incapable of eliciting; and his action thereby accomplishes the final catharsis necessary to Greek tragedy. By re-creating Thomas Sutpen as heroic protagonist of a classical drama, Mr. Compson effects a significant contrast to Miss Rosa's shadowy figure from Hell, which partakes of that hallucinatory aura enveloping the narrator who gives it shape.

The final re-creation of Thomas Sutpen is a composite product of two narrators, whose different backgrounds effect two extreme degrees of emotional involvement in the reconstruction of the legend. A southern birthright enables Quentin Compson to absorb the Sutpen story "without the medium of speech somehow from having been born and living beside it" (p. 212). To Quentin every person born in the South possesses a kind of Jungian "collective conscious-

[22]

ness," and hence a special insight into this land which gave him birth, because all are united by a common heritage that compels its descendants to look, not to the future, but forever backward into a shared past. To Shreve McCannon, the Canadian, the intellectual northerner separated by a thousand miles from Quentin's heritage, the young protagonist of *The Sound and the Fury* cries out: "You cant understand [the South]. You would have to be born there" (p. 361).

Cleanth Brooks classifies Shreve McCannon as the modern "liberal" twentieth-century reader "who is basically rational, skeptical, without any special concern for history, and pretty well emancipated from the ties of family, race, or section."[3] Unlike Quentin and Mr. Compson, Shreve does not inflate, and thus distort, the figures of the Sutpen myth because of an inherited patriotism which binds its "benefactors" to the shadowy heroes of a war that ended in 1865. Consequently his version is not a product of the southerner's emotional involvement in "tradition," for it is the interpretation of a narrator ignorant of the meaning, and thus the significance, of such a vague word.

Because it's something my people haven't got. Or if we have got it, it all happened long ago across the water and so now there aint anything to look at every day to remind us of it. We dont live among defeated grandfathers and freed slaves . . . and bullets in the dining room table and such, to be always reminding us to never forget. What is it? something you live and breathe in like air? a kind of vacuum filled with wraithlike and indomitable anger and pride and glory at and in happenings that occurred and ceased fifty years ago? a kind of entailed birthright father and son and father and son of never forgiving General Sherman, so that forevermore as long as your children's children produce children you wont be anything but a descendant of a long line of colonels killed in Pickett's charge at Manassas? (p. 361)

[23]

That Shreve, the "Northern, liberal intellectual," should narrate a tale in the tradition of southwest humor becomes, in light of the narrator's detachment, significant in itself. In direct contrast to Quentin, who is unable to disengage himself from the southerner's shared heritage, Shreve McCannon is the Canadian "emancipated from the ties of family, race or section," and thus the very genre he assumes is foreign to him. This last perspective, the viewpoint of the more impartial Canadian, is a very necessary one, for it adds control to an intensity that needs, at times, relief through contrast.

In this last composite re-creation of the Sutpen legend Shreve McCannon does most of the imaginative reconstruction. But he to a great extent retells the same story to Quentin that Quentin had earlier told him, in hopes that he might understand what motivates southerners to act as they do or even "why they live at all" (p. 174). Shreve's attitude gradually changes from one of ironic detachment to curiosity and then to utter amazement as Quentin narrates the genesis of Sutpen's design and Rosa Coldfield's "death" from outrage forty-four years before she was finally buried. However it is Quentin's presentation of the love drama—enacted by Judith, Henry, and Bon—that totally dissolves the invisible geographical boundary separating the Canadian from the southerner's world and actively involves him in the process of re-creation. By sharing youth's particular state of mind, Shreve and Quentin are able to tell the same tale, even to finish one another's thoughts—"both thinking as one, the voice which happened to be speaking the thought only the thinking become audible, vocal" (p. 303). This harmony of mind and feeling gradually deepens until it brings about an identification of Shreve and Quentin with the protagonists of their tale. The narrators, through a kind of transubstantiation by empathy, become

Charles-Shreve and Henry-Quentin—"now not two of them but four, the two who breathed not individuals now yet something both more and less than twins, the heart and blood of youth" (p. 294).

The tale told is a chivalric romance, celebrating the eternal verity of the love that inspired the songs of the troubadours. Faulkner, in one of his few authorial comments, reveals that Quentin, in re-creating the Sutpen legend, discards the false and conserves the true in what are to him the less important and less interesting aspects of the imagined story "in order to overpass to love" (p. 316). The reconstructed drama is threefold, with participants bound each to the other by the ties of the human heart: "the son who denied and repudiated, the lover who acquiesced, the beloved who was not bereaved" (p. 295).

For such a romantic tale the South's magnolias and soft summer nights provide the ideal backdrop. Although "the time had been winter in the [Sutpen] garden, and hence no bloom nor leaf even," Quentin prefers to re-create the flower-filled May morning conventional to the chivalric romance as the appropriate setting for the lovers, Judith and Charles: "The sister and the lover in the garden, pacing slowly, the sister's head bent with listening, the lover's head leaned above it while they paced slowly on in that rhythm which not the eyes but the heart marks and calls the beat and measure for, to disappear slowly beyond some bush or shrub starred with white bloom—jasmine, spiraea, honeysuckle, perhaps myriad scentless unpickable Cherokee roses" (pp. 294–95). To Quentin, as to the writers of the medieval romance, love—"where there might be paradox and inconsistency but nothing fault nor false" (p. 316)—is the origin of all good. In the literature of the Middle Ages love had an ennobling effect on the character of the lovers. Similarly, for Quentin and Shreve, Judith and Charles are sanctified

[25]

by their participation in this drama of love; they are elevated and become the protagonists of the medieval romance—the knight and his lady of the manor. Charles Bon is the "tragic Lancelot nearing thirty . . . sated with . . . experiences and pleasures." For Judith, the lady of high position, the princess imprisoned in the tower of Sutpen's Hundred, Bon's arrival in Mississippi is her "maiden meditative dream ridden up out of whatever fabulous land" (p. 320).

Bon, "the sybarite," wearing the soldier's "steel blade in the silken tessellated sheath" (p. 320), and Judith, "showing pride and honor about almost anything except love" (p. 341), are presented as the conventional courtly lover and his lady. Henry's role in the drama of three is actually that of intermediary between the lover and his lady, of confidant who brings Bon to Sutpen's Hundred and introduces him to Judith. However Quentin is the fictional storyteller who adapts the Sutpen story to the framework of the chivalric romance, and because of his relationship with Caddy (presented in *The Sound and the Fury*), he naturally identifies himself with Henry Sutpen. Because of this identification Henry—and not Charles Bon—becomes, in Quentin's narrative, the chivalric knight who must suffer and sacrifice in the service of love.

There are many conventions of courtly love which are repeated in the literature of the Middle Ages with such frequency that they become stereotyped. There are also many instances in which the genius of the medieval poet has transformed these commonplaces into something peculiarly his own. For example, in "The Complaint of Venus," Chaucer accomplishes an interesting change by letting the lady, and not the knight, praise the virtues of her lover; and in "The Complaint to his Empty Purse" the poet does not lament the coldness of his lady but the lightness of his purse. Faulkner similarly reshapes these conventions of the chivalric romance to the special nature of the tale he is telling. By juxtaposing Henry Sutpen's feelings for Charles Bon against the framework of the medieval romance, the artist emphasizes the ideal quality of the love and heightens the pathos of the act of fratricide. Thus, in Quentin's section, Henry is appropriately enough the courtly knight and the object of his reverence is Bon, who becomes to the impressionable provincial youth an idol, "a hero out of some adolescent Arabian Nights." As in the chivalric romance the object of the youth's admiration appears to be perfect in all attributes, praiseworthy both for comeliness and superior qualities of mind and heart. Bon is the "young man of a worldly elegance and assurance beyond his years, handsome, apparently . . . wealthy . . . a man with an ease of manner and a swaggering gallant air"; he is "the fine figure in the fine pants that fit his leg and the fine coats that fit his shoulders . . . that had more watches and cuff buttons and finer linen and horses and yellow-wheeled buggies . . . than most others did" (p. 304). In the presence of such a superior being, Henry exhibits the courtly lover's confusion and speechlessness and becomes "the clown," the "hobble-de-hoy" who "fumbled, groped, blurted with abrupt complete irrelevance" (p. 316) whenever he tried to express his admiration. Henry, the humble vassal, willingly submits to the reverential devotion and service that characterize chivalrous youth of all times. To Charles Bon, Henry desires to give "the humility which surrendered no pride—the entire proffering of the spirit of which the unconscious aping of clothes and speech and mannerisms was but the shell" (p. 317). Bon has only to tell Henry what to do and he will do it even though it appears dishonorable.

In addition to his idealized admiration for Charles Bon, Henry has a deep adoration for his sister Judith. His feelings toward both are expressed in his unfulfilled wish for "the pure and perfect incest"—a metamorphosing into the brother-in-law to despoil the sister and a metamorphosing into the sister who is despoiled by the brother-in-law. By virtue of the ennobling power of the shared love, Quentin translates the three of them—Henry, Bon, and Judith—"into a world like a fairy tale in which nothing else save them existed" (p. 318). This is the realm of courtly love; and the gods who preside over it, who "condone and practice . . . the dreamy immeasurable coupling" (p. 324), are merely a multiplication of the personified God of Love in medieval romance, who commands from the lover obedience to sensual pleasures.

Because of his close identification with the protagonist of his love drama, Quentin replaces the stereotyped emotions found in some chivalric romances with the sincere, genuine passion of the human heart, while employing at the same time the courtly commonplaces of this literary genre. The nature of the doomed situation makes a tragic ending inevitable: Judith loving Bon, unaware that he is her brother; Bon loving Judith, but willing to sacrifice this love in exchange for a silent touch of recognition from Sutpen, his father; and Henry loving both his sister Judith and his brother Bon and knowing that he must prevent their marriage. Tragedy is not uncommon to the chivalric romance; it shapes, among others, Chaucer's *Troilus and Criseyde* and the Knight's Tale, in which the conflict between love and friendship waged by the cousins Palamon and Arcite is strikingly parallel to Quentin's re-created drama. The tragedy in the Judith-Henry-Bon love story, as in *Troilus and Criseyde* and other chivalric romances ending unhappily, is brought about by Fortune, the capricious god who had a power arbitrarily to make one fall in love with anybody. Charles Bon is led by some deified force of folly to Judith Sutpen, thinking that she is *"a narrow delicate fenced virgin field*

*already furrowed and bedded so that all I shall need to do
is drop the seeds in"* (p. 326).

It is the convention of the medieval romance that the
lover must suffer for the sake of a love that is not easily
attainable, if attainable at all. Henry is the surrogate of the
fictional storyteller who shapes the tale to the chivalric romance, and he is thereby made to assume love's suffering
and service, which the passive fatalistic Bon renounces. Accordingly Henry must repudiate home and birthright for a
love he knows is doomed. "Holding . . . himself and Judith
and Bon in that suspension while he wrestled with his conscience to make it come to terms with what he wanted to
do" (p. 270), he, like the poet in Gower's incestuous tale
of Canace, must struggle to condone the unsanctioned relationship between brother and sister. When Henry answers
the "voices of his heredity and training which said *No. No.
You cannot"* (pp. 342–43) by citing to himself historical
examples of kings and other members of royalty who have
committed incest (one of whom is, appropriately enough,
the chivalric Duke John of Lorraine) in order to win his
conscience over to that which he desires, he engages in the
courtly lover's dispute between his Reason and his Will.
And when he finally allows Bon to write Judith, though he
knows such an act means the "irrevocable repudiation of the
old heredity and training and the acceptance of eternal
damnation" (p. 347), Henry makes it known that he is
willing to join the score of chivalric lovers before him who
have been sentenced to Purgatory—to that eternal "torment [in which] we will not need to remember love and
fornication" (p. 348)—for the service they performed for
love.[4] Although such men have "suffered for [love] and died
for it and are in hell now for it" (p. 343), Henry consoles
himself with the thought that "they still loved" (p. 342).
It is the element of miscegenation, however, that the south-

[29]

ern-doomed Henry and the young protagonist of *The Sound and the Fury* cannot repudiate—even for love. Although the final confrontation between the "two young embattled spirits" (p. 336), Bon and Henry, and the subsequent murder, presented as an act of "honor vindicated," partake of the conventions of the courtly romance, Faulkner has chosen to introduce the miscegenation motive into a tale of chivalry, and in so doing, he ingeniously reminds his audience that the drama, however romantic, is not of the long ago and faraway, but is a drama of the present and peculiarly of the South.

Quentin's narrative, shaped by the framework of the chivalric romance, represents a third significantly different way of interpreting the Sutpen story. For the young narrator the doom that envelops a family is neither the result of a demonic curse nor the hubris that destroyed the House of Atreus. Instead it becomes a "glamorous fatality," ennobling the participants who are condemned to suffer and sacrifice. In contrast to the two preceding perspectives centered around either a protagonist of a Satanic nature or one who, although heroic, has sacrificed to his design all "his soft virtues," Quentin conjectures that the annihilation of the entire line of Sutpen does not necessarily have to be divorced from love and honor and may even have these eternal verities as its cause.

It is only while Quentin and Shreve are re-creating the Judith-Henry-Bon story of universal love and youth's passion that the Canadian can suspend the skepticism of a non-southern, and hence "alien," consciousness in order to be able to finish Quentin's thoughts and sound like Mr. Compson (p. 261). In the reconstruction of the figure of Thomas Sutpen and his thirty-six-year invasion of Yoknapatawpha County, however, the northern intellectual is able to control his sympathies and his imagination's willing suspension of disbelief through cynicism and irony. Shreve's perspective is the fourth way of looking at Thomas Sutpen, and it is a very necessary one. This last point of view—without Quentin's and Mr. Compson's painfully mixed feelings regarding the region they live in, without Rosa's urgent desire to punish the man who "outraged" her—is, of the four perspectives, the least distorted because of an emotional involvement of the narrator in what he wishes to re-create.

Shreve McCannon's summary of Thomas Sutpen's story, from the time of his arrival in Jefferson in 1833 until his death in 1869, immediately follows Rosa Coldfield's ponderous recital of Sutpen's unearthly demonism in the italicized fifth chapter. The two perspectives are antithetical in tone—the one narrated by the storyteller most hopelessly involved with Sutpen, the other related by the narrator farthest away in time and space from the central figure of the legend. While Rosa's exaggerations, like those of Quentin and Mr. Compson, inflate the protagonist to greater-than-life size, Shreve's humorous exaggerations de-emphasize the importance of his actions in order to deflate Sutpen. The Canadian employs the same imagery used in the previous perspectives to describe Sutpen—Miss Rosa's phantom-demon, Mr. Compson's hero of the Greek tragedy. But in Shreve's narrative Sutpen's actions are neither Satanic nor heroic, and thus they fail to justify the magnitude of the protagonist. The result is the absurdly exaggerated "hero" of the tall tale in folk literature, patterned after the burlesques created by the Southwest humorists.

To the rational mind of the northerner the story of Sutpen and his dynasty appears to be beyond the realm of commonsense. The folk tale, with its gusty and often outrageous humor, is the only suitable literary genre to give shape to what is interpreted by the narrator as the absurd antics of an unbelievable group of people. Thus, in comparison to

Miss Rosa's phantom-villain demonically protected against harm from the Civil War's "bullet and ball" (p. 15) and Mr. Compson's Promethean demigod, the protagonist of Shreve's narrative becomes the shiftless creature from "Lubberland," frequently encountered in the pages of folk literature. Wearing beaver hat and "scuttling" down from the mountains of West Virginia "into respectability like a jackal into a rockpile" (p. 178), Shreve's figure of Sutpen—that "furious lecherous wreck" (p. 184), "haggling tediously over nickels and dimes with rapacious and poverty-stricken whites and negroes" (p. 182)—exhibits the traits of Lubberland's regional "hero," who falls somewhere between the wild and the civilized man on the ladder of cultural refinement. By comparing his imagined vision of Thomas Sutpen to a jackal, the detached northerner employs the comic simile of folk literature in which the character is related to an animal. As is often the case in the folk tales celebrating the unsophisticated man, Shreve presents his protagonist as an example of grotesque human behavior; and the events of the Sutpen story become for the first time ludicrous anecdotes about the fantastic men and women who people Quentin Compson's strange and alien world. Accordingly it is Shreve's viewpoint that relates the absurdly macabre burial of Thomas Sutpen: the fall of the corpse, dressed in "regimentals and saber and embroidered gauntlets" into a ditch; and the hasty extrication by the daughter who then "fetched him back to the cedar grove and read the service herself" (p. 186). This bizarre episode is an example of the southwestern writers' consistent use of graveyard humor, in which the depiction of death in its most exaggerated or grotesque forms is a source of laughter. And, by describing Bon's and Judith's engagement as contracted by an eager mother-in-law "almost before the fiance had had time to associate the daughter's name with the daughter's face"

[32]

(p. 327), the Canadian introduces into the love drama the element of the ridiculous and thereby destroys the seriousness essential to the chivalric romance. As in the folk tale, the individual is related to his culture. For Shreve the South is the macrocosm of Thomas Sutpen's design of greed, rapacity, and slaughter, and to the northerner it mirrors Sutpen's capacity for the outrageous. To the Canadian it is a land of "magnolias . . . and mockingbirds" and veterans, sporting "spurious bronze medals that never meant anything to begin with" (p. 328), who congregate on Decoration Day to celebrate a war lost fifty years ago by generals "as obsolete as Richard or Roland or du Guesclin" (p. 345), "who captured warships with cavalry charges but no grain nor meat nor bullets    who on one night and with a handful of men would gallantly set fire to and destroy a million dollar garrison of enemy supplies and on the next night be discovered by a neighbor in bed with his wife and be shot to death" (p. 346). This description of the burlesqued chivalric knight caught in an embarrassingly unexplainable dilemma is an example of the many off-color bawdy situations characterizing even the earliest documents of the southern frontier.

The tall tale may be defined as a folk tale which possesses transcendental overtones that enable the common man to assume exaggerated epic and cosmic proportions. Shreve, adopting the method peculiar to this literary genre of pushing the insignificant to an extreme degree of inflation, lifts his creations into the realm of the symbolic through comparison with legendary figures in literature, history, and mythology. To this he adds a sense of the outrageously grotesque heroic, related to the humor of the tall tale in folk literature. Sutpen, although "a mad impotent old man" motivated by lechery (p. 181), can become, in light of Mr. Compson's framework of the Greek tragedy, "a widowed

[33]

Agamemnon to [Rosa Coldfield's] Cassandra." When Shreve describes their courtship as taking place amid "unbidden April's compounded demonry" (p. 177), he employs the tall talk of folk literature—those purple passages of deliberate rhetorical overstatement—and thereby heightens the absurdly comical exaggeration. Like Rosa Coldfield's demon Shreve's figure of Thomas Sutpen is also a Faustus, whose "invulnerability was a part of the price he had got for whatever it was he had sold the Creditor, since according to the old dame he never had a soul" (p. 180). And, finally, Shreve's comparison of Sutpen to "the old Abraham full of years and weak and incapable now of further harm," whose "descendants increased an hundred fold as [his] soul goeth out" (p. 325), is an ironic and deliberately ludicrous contradiction of the Canadian's statement that the impotent old man was unable to breed a "batch of children" (p. 180).

The hero of Shreve's narrative—the demon, the Agamemnon, the Abraham—dies after the manner of the mortal hero in folk literature, a victim of a treacherous yet glorious death. The death implement, the rusty scythe that heretofore cut only vegetable weeds (p. 182), is also "deified" by the deed it does, and becomes "the symbolic laurel of a caesar's triumph" (p. 177). And when the murderer, Wash Jones—"this gangling malaria-ridden white man" (p. 183), this prime example of the illiterate clay-eater—is identified with "Shakespeare's very self" (p. 280), Shreve's farcical exaggeration reaches the extreme of humorous inflation.

What so outrages Shreve's rational mind is the discrepancy between the actual figure of Thomas Sutpen and the magnified figure that the three emotionally involved narrators choose to re-create. In an ingenious use of point-counterpoint, Shreve juxtaposes beside each tongue-in-cheek exaggeration of Sutpen a qualifying phrase or statement that deflates his previous inflation of the protagonist. Shreve is thereby able to depict the caricatured hero of the tall tale, whose celebrated feats of derring-do are discovered to be ridiculously exaggerated fabrications of the imagination. Accordingly the haunted castle of Rosa's perspective—standing "empty and unthreatening for twenty-six years and nobody [there] to meet or report any ghost" (p. 213)—can find, in Shreve's viewpoint, no more awesome goblin than Clytie, "a little dried-up woman not much bigger than a monkey" (p. 214), who is no longer Rosa Coldfield's Satanic watchdog or Mr. Compson's prophesying Cassandra, but "who might as well have been the ghost if one was ever needed" (p. 216). Similarly the Manfred of this doomed castle, Miss Rosa's Gothic villain, is, to the detached northern intellectual, no more fear-inspiring than "an ancient varicose and despairing Faustus" (p. 182) who finds it hard to realize "that there must be some limit even to the capabilities of a demon for doing harm" (p. 181). Moreover Shreve presents his interpretation of Sutpen's arrival in Jefferson as an obvious comic parody of Rosa Coldfield's description of the same event. Appearing "suddenly one Sunday with two pistols and twenty subsidiary demons," this "Faustus, this demon, this Beelzebub" is unable to live up to the demonry ascribed to him in Rosa's narrative. Thus, at the first "momentary flashy glare of his Creditor's outraged face exasperated beyond all endurance," Shreve's mock demon, this backwoods ring-tailed roarer—tucking "horns and tail beneath human raiment and a beaver hat" (p. 178)—decides the safest action lies in running. As much a diminished caricature of the tragic hero as Gothic villain, Shreve's Thomas Sutpen becomes, upon second thought, not an Agamemnon to Rosa's Cassandra, but instead an "ancient stiff-jointed Pyramus to her eager though untried Thisbe" (p. 177). Through this comic deflation of deep-

[35]

rooted symbols and legendary figures, Shreve heightens the outrageous humor of the tall tale.

With Shreve's perspective of Thomas Sutpen, the wheel, structurally speaking, comes full circle. The cynical and detached northerner utilizes the images of the earlier narratives to produce a different tone and mood. Through the ludicrous humor of the tall tale and through the use of dialect (found in all folk literature) to simulate the colloquial speech of Wash Jones, Jim Bond, and Thomas Sutpen, Shreve's viewpoint produces both a contrast to and control of the sustained seriousness and unrelieved hallucinatory tone found in Rosa Coldfield's narrative. In contrast to the preceding versions that exaggerate in order to inflate Sutpen, Shreve's narrative exaggerates to deflate a protagonist whose deeds seem to him to fall embarrassingly short of the mighty efforts of a classical hero or an immortal demon. If the preceding perspectives are guilty of distorting truth by overemphasizing the importance of what they recreate because of their narrators' emotional involvements in the South or in Thomas Sutpen, Shreve also distorts truth by overemphasizing the meaninglessness of the Sutpen story, by interpreting life, as it is lived in the South, as a cosmic joke, an unbelievable spectacle—and one "better than Ben Hur" (p. 217). Nevertheless these four perspectives, or as Faulkner says, "these thirteen different ways of looking at a blackbird," enable the reader to see a fourteenth image of Thomas Sutpen; and it is this fourteenth image that Faulkner said he liked to think is the truth (*Faulkner in the University*, p. 274).

When asked at Charlottesville about the accuracy of the four fictional narrators' respective re-creations of Thomas Sutpen, Faulkner made it quite clear that he himself conceived of Sutpen as a figure larger than life: "Taken all together, the truth is in what they saw though nobody saw the truth intact. So these are true as far as Miss Rosa and as Quentin saw it. Quentin's father saw what he believed was truth, that was all he saw. But the old man was himself a little too big for people no greater in stature than Quentin and Miss Rosa and Mr. Compson to see all at once" (*Faulkner in the University*, pp. 273–74). In *Absalom, Absalom!* Faulkner juxtaposes the story of Sutpen both with the story of King David in the Old Testament and with the framework of classical tragedy in order to endow with heroic proportions the protagonist of that novel in the Yoknapatawpha canon which is distinguished by its grand scale of character and action, its sustained intensity of tone and poetry of language.

The title of the novel is from Second Samuel; it is an ironic reference to the relationship of the half-brothers Absalom and Amnon and their father David of Israel to whom God promises that "thine house and thy kingdom shall be established for ever before thee: thy throne shall be established for ever" (2 Samuel 7.16). As Lennart Björk has pointed out, none of the analogues between *Absalom* and the passages in Second Samuel are clear-cut, "but the basic implications of the stories are identical."[5] For example Bon, who is denied filial recognition by Sutpen, corresponds not to Absalom, but to Amnon. Sutpen of course bears no resemblance from the point of view of character to the beneficent David, who holds sway over his kingdom not in order to establish his own name and tradition, but so that kingdom, established in God's name, might be enjoyed by all the children of Israel. As Hyatt Waggoner has observed, Sutpen—who appropriately enough christens his plantation "Sutpen's Hundred"—in this respect is much more like the "unjust builders" described in Psalm 49, who erect great estates in the hope of ensuring personal perpetuity by giving their names to their lands:[6] "Their [the doomed brutish people] inward thought *is, that* their houses *shall continue for ever, and* their dwelling places to all generations; they call *their* lands after their own names" (Psalm 49.11). That the analogies are not clear-cut, however, is not what is important. What is important is that Faulkner by means of thematic similarity—the concept of a dynasty, the threat of incest, the act of fratricide—and especially by means of the title itself is deliberately evoking the story of David, and by doing so he elevates the Sutpen legend through its juxtaposition with biblical myth.

In the thirteenth chapter of Samuel, as in *Absalom*, there is the theme of incest, as Amnon, David's son, falls in love with Absalom's sister Tamar. For sleeping with Tamar, Amnon is killed by Absalom, an act of fratricide which corresponds to Henry's shooting of Bon to prevent a similar union. In Samuel, as in *Absalom*, the act of fratricide threatens to leave David without an heir to his dynasty when Amnon's family cries out for retribution: "And, behold, the whole family is risen against thine handmaid, and they said, Deliver him that smote his brother, that we may kill him, for the life of his brother whom he slew; and we will destroy the heir also: and so they shall quench my coal which is left, and shall not leave to my husband *neither* name nor reminder upon the earth" (2 Samuel 14.7). Unlike Sutpen, in his relationship with Bon, David will forgive Absalom for killing his half-brother *because he is his son* (2 Samuel 14.11), just as he will later forgive him for joining Achitophel's unsuccessful rebellion. To Absalom, David can say the words which Thomas Sutpen will forever deny Charles Bon: "O my son Absalom, my son, my son Absalom! would God I had died for thee, O Absalom, my son, my son!" (2 Samuel 18.33).

Of the four narrators' individual versions of the Sutpen

[38]

story, Faulkner's own conception of the legend as a whole, from the point of view of scope and design, is most similar to Mr. Compson's—a drama possessing the simple heroic attributes of the characters in ancient Greek literature: "People too as we are, and victims too as we are, but victims of a different circumstance, simpler and therefore, integer for integer, larger, more heroic and the figures therefore more heroic too" (*Absalom, Absalom!*, p. 89). Years later at the University of Virginia Faulkner revealed that in conceiving the novel he was thinking of the Sutpen material in terms of classical tragedy: *Absalom* is the story, he said, of a man who wanted a line of princes and got too many, so that the "Greeks destroyed him, the old Greek concept of tragedy"[7] Faulkner's respect for the Greek tragedies is common knowledge, as they are included, along with *Don Quixote*, the Old Testament, and the writer's one-volume portable Shakespeare, in the list of books which he reread from time to time in order to find out, as he said, "a little more about truth" (*Faulkner in the University*, p. 50). It is interesting to note, however, that having been asked what book he would most like to have written and having answered *Moby-Dick*, Faulkner gives as reason for the choice the fact that Melville chose "the old simple clear Hellenic tradition" to tell his story of the sea: "The Greek-like simplicity of it: a man of forceful character driven by his sombre nature and his bleak heritage, bent on his own destruction and dragging his immediate world down with him with a despotic and utter disregard of them as individuals; the fine point to which the various natures caught (and passive as though with a foreknowledge of unalterable doom) in the fatality of his blind course are swept."[8] In Faulkner's praise of Melville's novel is his praise too of the old Greek plays, and the similarities which the southern writer sees between the two—the simplicity of plot, the presence of a central dominating figure who, in his drive toward self-fulfillment, brings about not only his own destruction but the destruction of those around him, the concept of Fate in the classical sense—are all found in his own novel which portrays the ruin of the doomed line of Sutpen.

In one of his discussions at the University of Virginia Faulkner interprets Aristotle's concept of tragedy as "man wishing to be braver than he is, in combat with his heart or with his fellows or with the environment, and how he fails, that the splendor, the courage of his failure, and the trappings of royalty, of kingship, are simply trappings to make him more splendid so that he was worthy of being selected by the gods, by Olympus, as an opponent, that man couldn't cope with him so it would take a god to do it, to cast him down." He then goes on to reveal that he saw Sutpen as fitting this conception of the old Greek hero: he was a man, Faulkner said, who "was going to take what he wanted because he was big enough and strong enough" (who, "given the occasion and the need . . . can and will do anything") and so was struck down by the gods and destroyed (*Faulkner in the University*, p. 51, 80–81). Cleanth Brooks sees Sutpen as "a heroic and tragic figure," and goes on to say that Faulkner's ability to create, in our times, "a character of heroic proportions and to invest his downfall with something like tragic dignity" is perhaps his most praiseworthy aspect (*The Yoknapatawpha Country*, p. 307). Brooks's accolade calls to mind Joseph Wood Krutch's questioning whether tragedy is possible in the twentieth century, since the modern audience is no longer capable of either a full appreciation of or identification with the heroic proportions associated with this genre. It is a tribute to Faulkner's genius as an artist that he has succeeded in creating a genuinely tragic protagonist in the classical sense; and indeed Thomas Sutpen seems the last of a line of heroic figures: "People too as we are . . . but simpler and therefore . . . larger, more heroic . . . not dwarfed and involved but distinct, uncomplex who had the gift of loving once or dying once instead of being diffused and scattered creatures drawn blindly limb from limb from a grab bag and assembled, author and victim too of a thousand homicides and a thousand copulations and divorcements."

In Greek literature the gods or fates rarely selected weak men for heroic destinies. The hero's inevitable tragic flaw, without which he would be able to master the hostile forces working both from within and from without—and which is ultimately the cause of his downfall—is also often inextricably associated with the strength which enables him to struggle or endure. Such is the case with Thomas Sutpen, whose continuing adherence to his design against insurmountable opposition is both his sin and the source of his grandeur. In distinguishing between Sutpen and Flem Snopes, Faulkner states the difference between the two in terms of their respective designs. Only in Sutpen's design is there something of heroic magnitude, he says, since that design represents a commitment to something both beyond and greater than the self: "Only Sutpen had a grand design. Snopes's design was pretty base—he just wanted to get rich, he didn't care how. Sutpen wanted to get rich only incidentally. He wanted to take revenge for all the redneck people against the aristocrat who told him to go around to the back door. He wanted to show that he could establish a dynasty too—he could make himself a king and raise a line of princes" (*Faulkner in the University*, pp. 97–98). If Sutpen is unable to force his entry into a clan, we know that he lacks no "failing of courage or shrewdness or ruthlessness" by which he will try to establish his own dynasty which will bear his name and tradition (p. 268). "He never did give up,"

General Compson tells Quentin, not without a touch of admiration for the old man's indefatigable spirit (p. 268). Even after Henry's act of fratricide destroys the hope of any heirs and after the Civil War destroys the plantation which is to be inherited by the progeny who no longer exist, Sutpen still believes he can "restore by sheer indomitable willing the Sutpen's Hundred which he remembered and had lost." In tribute to this indomitable will Wash Jones sees in "that furious lecherous wreck" still "the old fine figure of the man who once galloped on the black thoroughbred about that domain two boundaries of which the eye could not see from any point" (p. 184). *"A fine proud man,"* Wash thinks to himself. *"If God Himself was to come down and ride the natural earth, that's what He would aim to look like"* (p. 282).

As well as the source of his strength Sutpen's tenacity in his attempt to bring about the completion of his design is also his tragic flaw.[9] "He was amoral," Faulkner said of Sutpen at Charlottesville. "To me he is to be pitied, as anyone who ignores man is to be pitied, who does not believe that he belongs as a member of a human family, of the human family, is to be pitied" (*Faulkner in the University*, p. 80). The ultimate success of his design, not its moral implications, is what is important to Sutpen: "You see, I had a design in my mind," he tells General Compson. "Whether it was a good or a bad design is beside the point; the question is, Where did I make the mistake in it" (p. 263). Robert D. Jacobs names Sutpen as "the character in Faulkner who most nearly possesses *hubris.*" He goes on to say that the builder of Sutpen's Hundred makes "the most heroic effort of all Faulkner's characters to conquer time, not by suicide, nor by choosing his punishment, but by establishing a dynasty, the traditional way of the monarch."[10] If in this attempt to establish a dynasty, Sutpen engages in a more heroic mode of action, he is also guilty of the Greek hero's fatal sin of pride. By sacrificing to his design "his pity and gentleness and love"—by condemning, for the sake of an abstract dream, not just Charles Bon, but "all his blood . . . black and white both" (p. 269)—he defies the moral scheme of the universe. As in Greek tragedy he is struck down for his arrogance by the force of revenge. "Fate, destiny, retribution, irony" reduce the biggest landowner in Yoknapatawpha to a "furious lecherous wreck," "haggling tediously over nickels and dimes with rapacious and poverty-stricken whites and negroes" (p. 182). Jones, "who before '61 had not even been allowed to approach the front of the house" (a scene which must be juxtaposed to the young Sutpen's being prohibited from entering the plantation through the front door), now not only enters the house quite frequently (p.183), but helps Sutpen in running the country store. In order to bring about the tragic hero's fall, Fate (as Mr. Compson has pointed out) requires no less powerful a force than the Civil War; and so while Quentin listens to Miss Rosa recite the Sutpen story he realizes *why God let us lose the War: that only through the blood of our men and the tears of our women could He stay this demon and efface his name and lineage from the earth"* (p. 11).

Sutpen like the tragic hero refuses to make compromises that might save him from disaster. Theoretically he would have succeeded in accomplishing his grand design had he acknowledged Charles Bon as his son.[11] Bon asks only the single physical touch of recognition from Sutpen, and he will renounce Judith, he "will renounce love and all" (p. 327). The sign of recognition does not come, and the result is the fatal act of fratricide which deprives Sutpen of the line of princes to inherit the dukedom. At this point Sutpen appears to be divested of those heroic proportions which distinguish the tragic hero. In a frantic and doomed

[43]

race against time he is disappointed in his effort to produce a male heir, first when his attempted seduction of Rosa is unsuccessful and again when the offspring of his liaison with Wash's granddaughter Milly proves to be a girl, incapable of carrying on his name and lineage. Nevertheless at the moment of his death Sutpen's heroic stature is reaffirmed. Although he never recognizes the reason for the failure of the design, he does realize the fact of failure. This recognition prompts him to give the fatal insult to Milly, by which he succeeds in taunting Jones into killing him. In the manner of the Greeks and Elizabethans who deemed men courageous heroes as great as their doom, Faulkner accordingly elevates the scythe until it becomes "the symbolic laurel of a caesar's triumph" (p. 177). Wash Jones, in the scene in which he beheads Sutpen, becomes an almost allegorical figure of Time with his scythe; at the same time what is described is literally a decapitation—the death, as Jacobs perceptively observes, of a monarch (*Southern Renascence*, p. 189).

In keeping with his heroic theme, Faulkner employs in *Absalom, Absalom!* a literary style distinguished by its intensity of tone and poetry of language. The style, suitably adapted to the magnitude of the action presented, should be seen as the verbal correlative to a story which contains the elements of high tragedy—the powerful but doomed family, the action of incest, the slaying of brother by brother, the retributive punishment meted out by an avenging Fate.[12]

As Ilse Dusoir Lind points out, the fictional narrators speak in two voices—their own idiom, when they are engaged in casual conversation with one another, and the overall sound pattern of complex sentence structure and sustained rhetoric, when they are re-creating the legend of Sutpen.[13] It is significant that this is the exact stylistic

pattern found in classical tragedy: "Broadly speaking," says
J.A.K. Thomson, "there are two (and only two) styles in
[Greek tragedy]: the spoken and the sung, the dialogue and
the choruses. . . . All the characters in a Greek tragedy
express themselves, with minute shades of differentiation,
in the same style."[14] The second or more poetic style in
*Absalom* is of course consistent with the heroic associations
with which Faulkner has invested Sutpen, and the four
narrators, as they engage in re-creating the Sutpen legend,
themselves assume the role of the Greek chorus—chanting
Thomas Sutpen's arrival in Yoknapatawpha County "in
steady strophe and antistrophe: *Sutpen. Sutpen. Sutpen.
Sutpen.*" This elevated style is Faulkner's own equivalent
of the Greek choral odes or Shakespeare's blank verse; it is
not unlike Melville's rhetorical prose which sets apart the
tragic story of Ahab from the rest of the novel, and it is to
be purposefully differentiated from the more "realistic" dic-
tion generally found in the modern novel.[15]

While recognizing the tragic design of *Absalom, Absalom!* Melvin Backman concedes that he fails to find in the
novel the element of catharsis necessary to all Greek
tragedy. It is because Sutpen is not capable of self-awareness,
Backman says, and is thereby "incapable of purging from
himself the pride which forms the tragic element."[16] Thus
he concludes that Sutpen's life ends not in tragic affirmation
but in "unheroic death." It is true that Sutpen never does
realize his tragic flaw, and because he never experiences this
recognition, he fails to undergo that enlargement of spirit
by means of which the tragic hero triumphs over the consequences of his moral failings. As a result Sutpen's death is
without that tragic reconciliation to God and Nature's law
which, for example, attends both the dying Lear and the
aged and infirm Oedipus who learns what Sutpen never
does—that the gods strike down one who oversteps au-

thority. It is not Sutpen, but Quentin who, at the price of never again knowing a single moment of peace, realizes the injustice behind the design itself and, in so doing, experiences the recognition which can bring about a new order of things.[17] In his agonized cry as the novel ends is his realization of the enormous consequences of Sutpen's fatal sin, a sin which Quentin extends to include not just the doomed progenitor of Sutpen's Hundred but all the South.

Robert Jacobs calls Faulkner "perhaps the only writer of genuine tragedy today," and as reason for this statement he points specifically to the writer's belief in a moral universe: Faulkner "is a moralist of such fervor that the struggle between good and evil in his novels at its worst suggests a medieval allegory and at its best provides a tragic drama of titanic proportions" (*Southern Renascence*, pp. 171–72). The idea of a morally ordered universe in Faulkner is essentially a Greek view of life. Accordingly it is because Sutpen dared to defy this order that he had to be destroyed, as Faulkner himself pointed out: in his attempt to establish a dynasty, the writer said, "He violated all the rules of decency and honor and pity and compassion, and the fates took revenge on him" (*Faulkner in the University*, p. 35). Wash Jones kills Sutpen because he realizes in his inarticulate way that this man, whom in his authority and his courage he had once compared to God, had in his insult to Milly committed outrage against some basic law of justice. At this moment Wash, not unlike Quentin, extends Sutpen's guilt to include the entire South; he realizes the real reason that the South lost the war (and therefore in terms of the vast scheme of things was *destined* to lose the war) had nothing to do with economics or skill or even sheer numbers of combatants, but with morality. And so while he listens to the men gathering outside who will determine his punishment for murdering Sutpen, he sees in them the image of his old mentor: "Men

[46]

of Sutpen's own kind . . . men who had led the way, shown the other and lesser ones how to fight in battles . . . who had galloped also in the old days arrogant and proud on the fine horses about the fine plantations—symbol also of admiration and hope, instruments too of despair and grief . . . and maybe for the first time in his life he began to comprehend how it had been possible for Yankees or any other army to have whipped them" (pp. 289–90).

Sutpen's death—when seen from the point of view of the old Greeks—is not, as Backman argues, unheroic. Neither is it without a certain tragic affirmation. Every tragedy, Joseph Wood Krutch maintains, is an affirmation of faith in life, by virtue of its "satisfying the universally human desire to find in the world some justice, some meaning, or, at the very least, some recognizable order."[18] In classical tragedy the death of the hero, however catastrophic it might be, is justified, since that death is the means by which the conflict between good and evil is put to an end and universal harmony is restored. Such is the case in *Absalom, Absalom!* Listening to Quentin's tortured recital of his visit to Sutpen's Hundred, Shreve experiences, if only secondhand, the doom which attends insolence and pride. Though his tone is once again bantering, even sardonic, the Canadian accordingly predicts a new social order: "I think that in time the Jim Bonds are going to conquer the western hemisphere. Of course it won't quite be in our time. . . . But . . . in a few thousand years, I who regard you will also have sprung from the loins of African kings" (p. 378).

While the framework of *Absalom, Absalom!* is that of classical tragedy in general, Faulkner is also drawing on parallels from specific Greek plays. The Aristotelian theory of tragedy is particularly based on the *Oedipus Tyrannus* of Sophocles, as its many references to the play reveal, and in general thematic similarity *Absalom* also evokes the Oedipus cycle.[19] There are in both the elements of incest and the slaying of brother by brother; there is the presence of a curse which in both instances is brought about by the sins of the father and which is ultimately expiated only after the members of the family, or House, destroy one another. In addition there are the more specific analogies between Sutpen and Oedipus, Judith and Antigone, Sutpen's sons and Eteocles and Polyneices, with the double fratricide of Oedipus' sons echoed in *Absalom, Absalom!*

What has been said about the parallels between *Absalom* and the passages in Second Samuel can also apply to the Oedipus cycle—that the analogues are not always clear-cut, "but the basic implications of the stories are identical." For example not only does Sutpen fail to experience the classical hero's recognition of his tragic flaw, he does not even realize the fact that he sinned at all. When he asks General Compson, "Where did I make the mistake," he asks the question not in order that he might amend the injustice of his design, but so that through some adjustment in strategy he might still succeed in that design. Faulkner's protagonist accordingly never gains the knowledge that Oedipus has when he admits that "no other man has cursed me / I have brought down this curse upon myself";[20] and so in piecing together the Sutpen legend, Shreve wonders *"how* [Sutpen could] *be allowed to die without having to admit that he was wrong and suffer and regret it"* (p. 305). There is not with Sutpen, as there is with Oedipus, the feeling that he suffers more than he deserves, but neither is there any amelioration of Sutpen's punishment; his destruction is complete. Oedipus on the other hand is partially redeemed by virtue of his revelation and subsequent reconciliation to God and Nature's law. In *Oedipus at Colonus* the disgraced ex-ruler of Thebes becomes at his death a superhuman hero, able to

[48]

protect, from his grave, the Attic soil and worshipped for this power.

Although the analogies are not always clear-cut, the many instances of striking similarity between the story of Sutpen and the story of Oedipus indicate that Faulkner was purposefully drawing on Sophocles' trilogy in telling his own tale of the South. Sutpen like Oedipus fits Aristotle's definition of the tragic hero as a man "not pre-eminently virtuous and just," whose misfortune is brought about "not by vice and depravity but by some error of judgment." Specifically both are guilty of the fatal sin of pride. Consequently the recognition by the chorus at the end of the third episode of *Oedipus the King* that Oedipus' downfall has been brought about by pride, ambition, and presumption—those qualities which mark the tyrant—is not unlike Miss Rosa's realization of why Sutpen finally failed and was destroyed: *"I see . . . myself now: the accelerating circle's final curving course of his ruthless pride, his lust for vain magnificence, though I did not then"*(p. 162). In both the *Oedipus Tyrannus* and *Absalom* the pieces fit together like a detective story; the action centers around the true identity of Oedipus, the true identity of Charles Bon—and the repercussions of these discoveries. Again the protagonists wed in ignorance, and the knowledge of the consequences of this marriage, together with their tragic flaws, bring about their ultimate destruction. As the situation darkens, both Oedipus and Sutpen, confident of the efficacy of their own action, become more hopeful. When told he is not the son of Polybus and Merope—and when Jocasta realizes whose son he is—Oedipus claims he is still "the child of Fortune, giver of all good" (1. 1036). Similarly, after the war destroys Sutpen's Hundred, when Henry's murder of Bon removes the heirs from his union with Ellen Coldfield and when Miss

Rosa rejects the proposition which she deems antithetical to all she has ever been brought up to believe in, Mr. Compson surmises that Sutpen, now past sixty, *"was not for one moment concerned about his ability to start the third time"* (p. 278).

In both *Absalom* and the *Oedipus Tyrannus* the tragic deed is done within the family—"when murder is done by brother on brother, by son on father, by mother on son, or son on mother" (*Poetics*, p. 641). In Sophocles' play Oedipus himself kills his father and is indirectly responsible for his mother's death. In *Absalom* Sutpen destroys not just Bon, but Judith and Henry and Clytie too—"all his blood . . . black and white both." When Oedipus entrusts to Creon his daughters Antigone and Ismene, he realizes that they are fated "to waste away in barren maidenhood" (1. 1436) from their father's shame. This is Judith's destiny too. The line itself specifically calls to mind Rosa Coldfield when she tells Quentin it was Judith's fate to be "a widow without ever having been a bride" (p. 15). To the perpetrators of the familial curse the punishment is the same. Sutpen in losing his heirs is also deprived of his dynasty, the distinguishing mark, as Jacobs has pointed out, of the monarch. Similarly, to the exiled Oedipus, Creon proclaims that "Nothing can restore / Your old dominion. You are King no more" (11. 1457–58).

The identification with the line of Oedipus is carried over into the second generation. By means of deliberate association with Oedipus' offspring—Antigone, Eteocles, and Polyneices, Faulkner heightens the tragic aspect of the Judith-Henry-Bon subplot. Though more passive than the vengeful elder son of Oedipus, Bon corresponds in the threefold drama to Polyneices. Both are cursed by their fathers —Polyneices literally in the climactic scene of *Oedipus at Colonus*, Bon less overtly and more cruelly when Sutpen denies him filial recognition. Polyneices' being stripped of his kingship and banished in exile from Thebes parallels Sutpen's refusal to acknowledge Bon as his son, thereby depriving him of the opportunity of ever inheriting the dynasty. Both attempt to regain the rightful possession of their home—Polyneices by storming Thebes, Bon in a more peaceful way by the choice he gives Sutpen: either the sign of recognition or the marriage with Judith. It is in this attempt to regain what is theirs that both meet death at the hands of a brother. If Bon in many respects corresponds to Polyneices, Henry has as his analogue in the Oedipus trilogy Eteocles, the younger brother. Henry, like Eteocles who defends the land which Polyneices attacks, protects both Judith and the Sutpen lineage from Bon's threat of miscegenation: to Henry's passionate cry of "Brother," Bon taunts, *"No I'm not. I'm the nigger that's going to sleep with your sister. Unless you stop me, Henry"* (p. 358). Like Eteocles, Henry, in his effort to protect the dynasty, is forced to kill his brother, and like Eteocles he is for all purposes destroyed by this act of fratricide. To the listening Quentin, Rosa Coldfield describes Henry's destiny: he was "the son who . . . repudiated the very roof under which he had been born and to which he would return but once more before disappearing for good, and that as a murderer and . . . a fratricide" (p. 15).

Cleanth Brooks calls Judith Sutpen "one of Faulkner's finest characters of endurance." He goes on to say that she endures "not merely through numb, bleak Stoicism but also through compassion and love. Judith is doomed by misfortunes not of her making, but she is not warped and twisted by them. Her humanity survives them" (*The Yoknapatawpha Country*, p. 319). The qualities for which Brooks praises Judith—courage and compassion and devotion—are also exhibited by Sophocles' Antigone; more significantly their respective stories are strikingly parallel. For both Antigone and Judith all their evils are bequeathed to them by their fathers, and yet they continue to show complete filial devotion and service. In *Oedipus at Colonus*, the action of which follows twenty years after *Oedipus the King*, Antigone continues to care for the blind and aged Oedipus, just as Judith still cares for Sutpen after the war and after the death of her fiancé, even helping him to run the crossroads store. In both cases an undesired marriage is prevented by death. By decreeing death to Antigone, Creon successfully breaks up the proposed wedding between her and his son Haemon, who then kills himself. Creon's "Death will act for me. Death will stop the marriage"[21] is Sutpen's attitude too as the builder of Sutpen's Hundred passively waits for either the Civil War or Henry to remove Charles Bon, who as suitor to Judith threatens the continuation of the dynasty. In *Antigone* Sophocles' heroine is compared to her sister Ismene, and shown to be superior by virtue of her courage. Ismene dares not provoke Creon's wrath by defying his edict which refuses burial to Polyneices: "But to challenge / Authority—I have not strength enough" (11. 77–78). Antigone, on the other hand, will dare to challenge authority for the sake of love. She ministers the appropriate rites of burial to her brother, and the act costs her her life. Similarly Judith is compared to Henry, and like Antigone she is the one who possesses the attribute of courage: of the two children Judith was "the Sutpen with the ruthless Sutpen code of taking what it wanted provided it were strong enough." Judith thought, *"If happy I can be I will, if suffer I must I can"* (pp. 120–21). Like Antigone the grieving Judith is the one who buries the rejected brother. Unlike Antigone she dies not in ministering to her own family, but to Charles Bon's— specifically by nursing Bon's son when he is stricken with yellow fever. It is at this point that she, like the equally compassionate Antigone, dares to challenge authority. In nursing Bon's son, Judith, as Brooks has stated, acknowledges the kinship of blood and, in so doing, repudiates Sutpen's design—an act which Henry is never capable of performing.

Jacobs sees in the figure of Henry Sutpen a striking similarity to Orestes—"a fratricide and fugitive, pursued by the Erinyes of his own conscience" (*Southern Renascence*, p. 188). Certainly both have this in common—that they are unwilling instruments of revenge who are used by one more dominating member of their family to slay another member of that family. The punishment for the act of murder is the same: as the curse of his mother's blood cuts Orestes off from the home of his father, so Henry's slaying of his own kin prevents him from inheriting Sutpen's Hundred. That Faulkner had in mind not only the Oedipus cycle but also the tragedy of the House of Atreus and that he was drawing on this analogue in *Absalom, Absalom!* is made apparent by the particular name he gives to Sutpen's Negro daughter. Mr. Compson tells Quentin that Sutpen called her Clytemnestra, though he himself prefers to believe that he intended to name her Cassandra "to designate the presiding augur of his own disaster" (p. 62).

It is possible that the burning of Sutpen's Hundred has as its source the scene in Euripides' *Orestes* in which Pylades and Electra set fire to Agamemnon's palace. In both *Absalom* and *Orestes* what is being burned is the royal seat of the dynasty and in both the motive for setting the fire is the same. If Orestes and Electra fail to kill Helen (an act of retribution for Menelaus' failure to aid them when on trial for matricide), they will then set fire to their palace and kill themselves in "honourable escape." This too is Clytie's reason for burning Sutpen's Hundred. Mistaking the approaching ambulance which in reality has come to save

[53]

Henry for the police wagon "which will carry [him] into town for the white folks to hang," she kindles the stored kerosene and tinder in order to give to Sutpen's last surviving son the same honorable escape: "Whatever he done," she says, "me and Judith and him have paid it out" (p. 370). Both Euripides' play and Faulkner's novel end with the purgation of the doomed house. The final description of the collapse of Sutpen's Hundred, with Rosa frantically struggling with the deputies but making no sound, her face lit by the crimson reflection of the burning house, and only the howling of the idiot left—the sole survivor of the Sutpen line—is, as George Marion O'Donnell says, "as nearly a genuine tragic scene as anything in modern fiction."[22] It is fitting that Sutpen's Hundred—the concrete representation of its builder's monstrous sin—should be destroyed by fire, for it suggests an unconscious act on Clytie's part of purification: "The tragic gnome's face beneath the clean headrag, against a red background of fire, seen for a moment between two swirls of smoke, looking down at them, perhaps not even now with triumph and no more of despair than it had ever worn, possibly even serene above the melting clapboards before the smoke swirled across it again" (p. 376). The emotions of pity and fear are finally reconciled and replaced by the affirmative feeling of peace. What is being dramatically rendered is the catharsis of the Greek play, the necessary element which ends all genuine tragedies.

# CHAPTER III

# Faulkner's Use
# of Epic and Myth

The final section of *The Hamlet* bears the title "The Peasants"; it is an evocation of Balzac's *Comédie Humaine*, that Herculean literary effort to see in the contemporaneous and in the ordinary the universal human condition. Faulkner opens *The Hamlet* with a description of the people who settled Frenchman's Bend, and in many respects it is sociologically and economically representative of the southern frontier society in general at the time of the coming of the plantation:

They came from the Atlantic seaboard and before that, from England and the Scottish and Welsh Marches, as some of the names would indicate—Turpin and Haley and Whittington, McCallum and Murray and Leonard and Littlejohn, and other names like Riddup and Armstid and Doshey which could have come from nowhere since certainly no man would deliberately select one of them for his own. They brought no slaves and no Phyfe and Chippendale highboys; indeed, what they did bring most of them could (and did) carry in their hands. They took up land and built one- and two-room cabins and never painted them, and married one another and produced children and added other rooms one by one to the original cabins and did not paint them either, but that was all. Their descendants still planted cotton in the bottom land and corn along the edge of the hills and in the secret coves in the hills made whiskey of the corn and sold what they did not drink. Federal officers went into the country and vanished. Some garment which the missing man had worn might be seen—a felt hat, a broadcloth coat, a pair of city shoes or even his pistol—on a child or an old man or woman. County officers did not bother them at all save in the heel of election years. They supported their own churches and schools, they married and committed infrequent adulteries and more frequent homicides among themselves and were their own courts, judges and executioners. They were Protestants and Democrats and prolific; there was not one Negro landowner in the entire section. Strange Negroes would absolutely refuse to pass through it after dark. (pp. 4–5)

Because it is very representative, Frenchman's Bend, Faulkner's rich riverbottom country lying twenty miles southeast of Jefferson, his county seat, might be any provincial southern community, a kind of backwoods "Main Street" in the third decade of the century. Hill-cradled and remote, it is given its boundary on one side by the gutted shell of the Old Frenchman's Place. Its center is the crossroads store and cotton gin owned and operated by Will Varner. Shrewd in business and of a Rabelaisian turn of mind, Varner at sixty has already fathered sixteen children on his wife and is still lusty; he is "the chief man of the country," Frenchman's Bend's farmer, usurer, veterinarian in one. Spreading out from the general store and cotton gin and on into the hills are the small farms, some owned outright by and many mortgaged to Varner. In the grassless yard adjoining the village's livery barn Mrs. Littlejohn runs the rambling "half-log half-sawn plank" hotel where drummers and livestock-traders are fed and lodged. Nearby Ben Quick operates the sawmill; Trumbull tends to his chores as blacksmith. There are always a dozen or so overalled men squatting about the gallery of Varner's store with pocketknives and slivers of wood, bawdy jokes and the latest gossip. Making the rounds

[56]

of Frenchman's Bend is the sewing-machine agent, V. K. Ratliff, who travels Beat Four with his team and with his painted dog kennel which is just large enough to carry one demonstration sewing machine neatly inside. Affable and garrulous, Ratliff loves the house-to-house communion as much as the commission, and so he carries with him not only the sewing machines but the "personal messages from mouth to mouth about weddings and funerals and the preserving of vegetables and fruit with the reliability of a postal service" (p. 13). Frenchman's Bend even has its own town eccentric. Uncle Dick Bolivar, so old that "he antedated everyone," lives in the mud-daubed hut in the riverbottom without any kin and without any ties. He takes time out from selling his charms and his nostrums to help Ratliff and Armstid and Bookwright on their ill-fated venture by sounding, with his plumbline of string and tobacco sack, for buried treasure on the Old Frenchman's Place.

Part of *The Hamlet* is given over to the tall tale as portrayed in the best tradition of the southwestern humorists. The auction of the spotted horses and the Pat Stamper material could have come straight out of the pages of A. B. Longstreet. Both incidents are full of the gusty, often outrageous humor of the folk tale; they are, in fact, exactly the kind of yarns Ratliff would love to spin, and so it is quite fitting he should narrate how Ab Snopes got "soured" in a horse swap with the master, Pat Stamper, "a legend, even though still alive" (p. 30). No ordinary horse trade, this; to Ab "the entire honor and pride of the science and pastime of horse-trading in Yoknapatawpha County [was] depending on him to vindicate it" (p. 35). Ratliff loves to embellish a story, and we can feel him savoring the fine points on which the duping turns—Ab trading Stamper the cream separator which Mrs. Snopes had patiently saved her nickels and dimes for until she got the $24.68 to buy it; Ab getting back for the cream separator the same scrawny bay-colored horse he had started out with that morning, only now painted black and inflated with a bicycle pump; Mrs. Snopes trading in return for the separator her only cow and thus her only source of milk. The frenzied odyssey of the wild Texas ponies is every bit as outrageous. With heads shaped like ironing boards, and calico bodies the color of "pieces of circus posters," they break loose from the corral and whip about the countryside "like dizzy fish in a bowl" (p. 279). One runs inside Mrs. Littlejohn's boarding house, crashes into her melodeon, then surprises V. K. in his bedroom. Both quickly exit—he out the window, the horse by the back porch. The Pat Stamper horse trade and the odyssey of the Texas ponies have the elements of folk literature. Certainly it is not out of place in *The Hamlet,* for it is a genre indigenous to and highly enjoyed by the type of rural hill people who are portrayed here.

In the midst of the daily routine of Frenchman's Bend, occasionally highlighted by such activities as the romp of the Texas horses, there is, however, something wondrous going on. Over the same land where the pink Texas ponies run wild, where Mink Snopes laboriously works for fifty cents a day to pay Houston for wintering his cow, the idiot Ike Snopes wanders with his cow in a fantastic love idyll, like some courtly knight out of medieval romance. Here too Flem Snopes mysteriously appears one day with his father Ab from out of America's mythical "West" (p. 8) to snatch away Eula Varner, Frenchman's Bend's Helen of Troy, in a bizarre reenactment of Pluto's rape of Persephone. There is nothing ordinary about these three. Ike, Flem, and Eula are all larger than life, and whatever world they relate to has little to do with the mundane day-to-day routine of Frenchman's Bend. One distinction which the three have in common is that they are all remarkable for their silence in the

[58]

novel—a silence which makes them something beyond ordinary human beings. Ike only speaks in *The Hamlet* when he tries to answer I. O.'s cruel prodding to make him say his name. "Ike H-mope," he says; and again, "Ike H-mope" (p. 87). It comes out slowly and pathetically. The fact that Ike is an idiot of course explains his inarticulateness. And yet the long poetic reverie in which dawn is discovered to be not light reflected onto the earth from the sky, but instead suspired from the earth itself, is presented as Ike's imaginative construction of the universe. Logically, of course, Ike is incapable of such a vision, but the point is that we go along with it—that this would be the idiot's perception of the world around him if he could articulate such a perception—just as we go along with Faulkner's transformation of Ike into a contemporary courtly knight who is so transformed because he is brave enough to defend the object of his love from water, fire, and "dragon."[1] Michael Millgate has pointed out that Flem speaks only 244 words in the novel.[2] Because of his single-minded purpose of taking over all of Jefferson and because of the efficacy with which he brings about such a purpose, Flem hardly appears human. Rather he seems more the personification of the power of absolute evil, an identification which is strengthened by Ratliff's reverie of Flem in Hell. After the reverie cosmic forces have entered into Frenchman's Bend, and we can never again see Flem simply as an aggrandizing hill farmer. Eula speaks three times in *The Hamlet*—once when she brings McCarron home after the ambush, and again when her family discover she is pregnant. She also answers Labove's abortive attempt to rape her, and it lets the schoolteacher know she has at least learned one thing in the five years she has been in his classroom: "Stop pawing me," she reprimands him. "You old headless horseman Ichabod Crane" (p. 122). The extraordinary beauty who is unaware

[59]

of her power over men is first transformed in *The Hamlet,* by virtue of this power, into a principle of fertility and is then further elevated into the more heroic world of myth and becomes a goddess. Ratliff recognizes that Eula is partially distinguished by her silence, and in this respect he compares her to Helen of Troy, who, he imagines, unlike the Semiramises and Judiths and Liliths and Francescas and Isoldes, never talked either, and so never destroyed her mystery by explaining it: "But not like Helen. Not that bright, that luminous, that enduring. It's because the others all talked. They are fading steadily into the obscurity of their own vocality within which their passions and tragedies took place. But not Helen. Do you know there is not one recorded word of hers anywhere in existence, other than that one presumable Yes she must have said that time to Paris?" (*The Mansion,* p. 133).

In his discussions at Charlottesville Faulkner himself has said that Eula Varner was a figure beyond the ordinary, a little too glorious for her contemporary provincial surroundings to satisfy or even to contain. "She was larger than life," he said. "That she was an anachronism, she had no place there, that that little hamlet couldn't have held her, and when she moved on to Jefferson, that couldn't hold her either" (*Faulkner in the University,* p. 31). In *The Hamlet* Eula is indeed an anachronism, marching to the beat of different drums: "She seemed to be not a living integer of her contemporary scene, but rather to exist in a teeming vacuum in which her days followed one another as though behind sound-proof glass." The world to which Eula really belongs is the older heroic world of pagan mythology, and the men of Frenchman's Bend, by some incredible freak of nature, have earned the privilege of seeing, at this particular moment in history, on this one geographical spot out of all the world, what a goddess was really like, for "her entire

appearance suggested some symbology out of the old Diony-
sic times—honey in sunlight and bursting grapes, the
writhen bleeding of the crushed fecundated vine beneath
the hard rapacious trampling goat-hoof" (p. 95). Eula is born
unbelievably beautiful. She reaches maturity at an incredibly
early age, "already grown at eight, who apparently had
reached and passed puberty in the foetus" (p. 114); and she
radiates from that "body which seemed always to be on the
outside of its garments" (pp. 121–22) a great seductive
power, while at the same time she remains unconscious of
that power. Eula is also "incorrigibly lazy." She spends her
first years in a perambulator until it takes the strength of
a grown man to lift her out of it. She is persuaded to leave
her carriage only by the promise of a graduation to chairs.
Far from being the flaw that makes her human, however,
Eula's inertia complements Faulkner's presentation of her
as feminine principle par excellence, so that the scene in
which the six-year-old Eula, in the company of her mother,
is carried by the Varner's Negro manservant—staggering
slightly beneath "his long, dangling, already indisputably
female burden"—becomes, very appropriately, the "bizarre
and chaperoned" reenactment of the "Sabine rape" (p. 96).

The test of Eula's extraordinary power comes with the
entry of Labove into Frenchman's Bend. A product of "his
dirt-farmer tradition and heritage," Labove, at the cost of
a great deal of personal sacrifice and a lot of hard work, is
a young man determined to rise above his background and
become governor. While he pursues his goal with an almost
fanatic intensity, he possesses many admirable qualities: he
is a man of deep integrity capable of remarkable self-disci-
pline. Squeezing the work of four years into three, he earns
a double degree at the state university by playing on the
school's football team for six Saturdays every fall (the game
enables him to supply his poor-white family, including his

great-grandmother, with cleated football shoes which he will take from his athletic locker only when his team wins), by working in the sawmill, and by traveling the forty miles to Jefferson each Sunday on horseback to fulfill his duties as Will Varner's new schoolmaster, a chore he performs when he is not either planting or harvesting the farming crop for his own family. While other youths pursue the pleasures which are also a part of university life, Labove is the ascetic who a thousand years before, Faulkner tells us, would have been a monk, "a militant fanatic who would have turned his uncompromising back upon the world with actual joy" (p. 106); he has the "hill-man's purely emotional and foundationless faith in education, the white magic of Latin degrees, which was an actual counterpart of the old monk's faith in his wooden cross" (p. 118).

Labove's undoing is that circumstance or fate has conspired against him and ordained that Eula Varner be one of his pupils. At that instant when he first turns around from the blackboard to see the eight-year-old girl "with the body of fourteen and with the female shape of twenty," there intrudes into the small, poorly-heated room which is dedicated to the stern and strict teaching of Protestant primary education "a moist blast of spring's liquorish corruption, a pagan triumphal prostration before the supreme primal uterus" (p. 114). Eula transforms Labove's wooden desks and benches "into a grove of Venus"; she makes every male in that room, from children to grown men, battle one another for "precedence in immolation" (p. 115). Three years later the schoolteacher has become totally bewitched; he sees the figure of the eleven-year-old Eula sitting on the schoolhouse steps at recess, eating a cold potato, as "one of the unchaste and perhaps even anonymously pregnant immortals eating bread of Paradise on a sunwise slope of Olympus" (p. 124). Labove himself admits that he has become quite mad. It is an obsession that has now affected his mind as well as his body. Even after he is admitted to the bar he cannot leave Jefferson, for in doing so he would leave behind the cause of both his ecstasy and his torment; what the schoolteacher realizes is that the price of the three years of sacrifice and endurance has not bought so much the anticipated degrees as it has "the privilege of dedicating his life" to Will Varner's daughter (p. 122). As homage to the power of her presence Labove transforms all who come into close contact with Eula into minor deities to that one commanding Venus. To Labove, Jody is "the jealous seething eunuch priest" (p. 115) who takes Eula home from school —and thus away from him. The schoolteacher mysteriously and quite correctly divines her future husband, the recipient of all that glory: "He would be a dwarf, a gnome, without glands or desire. . . . The crippled Vulcan to that Venus, who would not possess her but merely own her by the single strength which power gave." Labove is himself finally transformed. Because of his obsession the monk becomes a satyr, with "his legs haired-over like those of a faun." Labove briefly thinks of marrying Eula, but then he realizes that he wants to possess her just once "as a man with a gangrened hand or foot thirsts after the axe-stroke which will leave him comparatively whole again" (p. 119). He makes that one abortive attempt to rape her and is embarrassingly rebuked ("Stop pawing me, you old headless horseman Ichabod Crane"). When the schoolteacher realizes that Eula did not tell Jody of the rape attempt because "she doesn't even know anything happened that was worth mentioning" (p. 127), Labove locks his schoolhouse door for the last time, hangs the key on the nail outside, and leaves Jefferson forever.

Argument could be made that Eula's presentation as pagan divinity is the result of her character's being shaped by the obsessed imagination of a classical scholar—that Labove would by choice or necessity see in her the quality of "the very goddesses in his Homer and Thucydides" (p. 114), and indeed Faulkner himself has warned that it was his books that had already betrayed Labove. But in one of his few intrusions in the novel, Faulkner describes Frenchman's Bend as "a little lost village, nameless, without grace, forsaken, yet which wombed once by chance and accident one blind seed of the spendthrift Olympian ejaculation and did not even know it" (p. 149). What is significant is that it is the author speaking and not Labove. The same desire and frustration which Eula unleashes in Labove's classroom she also inspires in the swains of Frenchman's Bend who gather each Sunday on Varner's porch, each vainly trying to sit the other out, like bees swarming to get to "that center . . . the queen, the matrix" (p. 116). Moreover Labove might transform Jody into Eula's attendant eunuch and Flem into her crippled Vulcan, but it is Faulkner who transforms Labove into the satyr. There is also the matter of the mysterious drought which settles over Frenchman's Bend and exactly coincides with that time period in which Flem, having married Eula, takes her away from Yoknapatawpha County. Faulkner makes it known that it is no ordinary dry spell. This was the time that "ancient Lilith" reigned once again, the extraordinary "fall before the winter from which the people as they became older were to establish time and date events" (p. 263). The point is that the whole universe is somehow involved with Eula. That the return of spring should exactly coincide with Eula's return to the Bend—"all coming at once, pell-mell and disordered, fruit and bloom and leaf, pied meadow and blossoming wood and long fields shearing dark out of winter's slumber, to the shearing plow" (p. 269)—evokes the myth of Persephone and specifically her rape by the god of the underworld.

[64]

In his excellent discussion of *The Hamlet* Brooks sees Eula as the representative of the feminine principle "in an almost chemically pure form." She would be a parody of femininity, he continues, if Faulkner had not managed to make her such a convincing goddess: "The truth of the matter," Brooks states, "is that Eula is at once caricature and goddess, for in his treatment of her Faulkner does not let his sense of humor desert him" (*The Yoknapatawpha Country*, p. 190). There is in the course of *The Hamlet*, however, a significant and profound change in Eula. It comes at that moment when her father arranges the contractual marriage with Flem. When Ratliff sees her for the first time after her Texas honeymoon, sitting in the surrey and holding her tiny baby daughter, he notices especially "the beautiful face . . . [as] it passed in profile, calm, oblivious, incurious. It was not a tragic face: it was just damned" (p. 270). It is Ratliff who laments the terrible waste—not just wasted on Snopes, he thinks, "but on all of them, himself included": "the splendid girl with her beautiful masklike face" wed to "the froglike creature" (p. 149). It is at this point that Eula is no longer a source for humor, and yet in her defeat she is still larger than life. When V. K. goes to summon Will Varner to care for the injured Henry Armstid, after Armstid has broken his leg trying to capture his Texas pony, he looks up to see Eula at the window, looking out on the night: "She was in a white garment; the heavy braided club of her hair looked almost black against it. She did not lean out, she merely stood there, full in the moon, apparently blank-eyed or certainly not looking downward at them—the heavy gold hair, the mask not tragic and perhaps not even doomed: just damned, the strong faint lift of breasts beneath marblelike fall of the garment; to those below what Brunhilde, what Rhinemaiden on what spurious river-rock of papier-mâché, what

Helen returned to what topless and shoddy Argos, waiting for no one" (p. 311). The bucolic goddess has been transformed into a Valkyrie, a figure worthy now of tragedy. Like the tragic protagonist in the old classical sense, Eula, no longer the passive feminine principle, is now capable of performing the heroic act. When she takes her life in *The Town* it is to protect Linda's good name, "to leave her child a mere suicide for a mother instead of a whore" (*The Town*, p. 340). It is an act which wins her one more admirer. In *The Mansion* Ratliff builds for posterity what he calls "The Eula Varner room." In it he has placed the seventy-five dollar Allanovna necktie under a glass bell and an Italian piece of sculpture by Linda's husband Barton Kohl. It is a shrine set up by Frenchman's Bend, he tells Gavin Stevens, and the fact that "shrine" and not "monument" is just the right word he wishes to use indicates that to Ratliff also Eula is a little too great, a little too special to be judged against ordinary human standards. "When a community is lucky enough," he says, "to be the community that every thousand years or so has a Eula Varner to pick it out to do her breathing in, the least we can do is for somebody to set up something. . . . A shrine to mark and remember it, for the folks that wasn't that lucky, that was already doomed to be too young" (p. 232).

If in his creation of Eula Varner Faulkner has allowed Frenchman's Bend the privilege of experiencing once again how splendid the pagan goddesses must have been, he has, in his presentation of Flem Snopes, also reminded them that the world once believed in demons. Flem stands apart from all of the writer's villains because Faulkner chooses to give no logical explanation, in terms of human motivation, of why he acts out of pure evil. We are never allowed inside his mind. Speaking only those 244 words (plus the additional thirty-three V. K. imagines his saying in the scene in Hell),

[66]

Flem silently but very effectively goes about his single-minded purpose of acquiring first money and then power, epitomized by his mansion and the appointment as president of the bank of Jefferson. He becomes a force of evil, outside the human community; and so his stance as he watches the auction of the spotted Texas horses is symbolic: "Standing there in his small yet definite isolation" (p. 297), Flem appears to be merely a bystander as he watches Buck Hipps dupe the Bend into buying the crazy poster-colored ponies that they cannot even catch. But it is not Buck but Flem who refuses to give back to Mrs. Armstid the five dollars she earned by weaving at night, and thus we know the Texan is only his instrument, and he the mastermind behind the plot.

Flem's pursuit and capture of Yoknapatawpha County as "his domain, his barony" (*The Mansion*, p. 219) has, it appears, more than a little in common with Thomas Sutpen's attempt to establish his dynasty. But Sutpen's Hundred was originally conceived from a most noble and praiseworthy motive—as a West Virginia mountaineer's protest against that particular state of affairs which sanctions one man's ordering another to go around to the back door simply because he is of a different social class. Because Sutpen is acting not out of simple greed, but for a cause he deems greater than himself, he achieves a certain heroic stature and prompted Faulkner to name him one of his most nearly perfect tragic characters (*Faulkner in the University*, p. 119). Flem also has something in common with Popeye, the sinister figure in *Sanctuary*. Both men are impotent, a condition which prevents any normal relationship with women and, by extension, with the human race. But while Flem, as a personification of evil, is a force larger than life, Popeye is something less than human, and he is accordingly presented in terms of animal imagery throughout the novel. Faulkner also chooses to give, at the end of *Sanctuary*, the long account of Popeye's heredity and early home environment, and so affords the "naturalistic" explanation of why Popeye is like he is. Perhaps that Faulknerian villain with whom Flem, in terms of sheer "out and out meanness," has most in common is Jason Compson, and Faulkner himself indicates he thinks of them together when he states that they are the two characters he has created who are "completely inhuman" (*Faulkner in the University*, p. 132). Both pursue their rapacious drive after wealth without compunction or conscience; both are guilty too of a more heinous sin—a diabolic cruelty toward the members of their own family. As he did with Popeye, however, Faulkner chooses to explain why Jason intercepts Caddy's checks to Quentin and in the explanation indicates that he, like Ab, has become "soured." Jason has never forgiven Caddy for her "indiscreet" pregnancy, for it is the cause of Herbert Head's divorcing her, and the action ends Jason's dream of the promised job in the bank. His niece, then, had had no "entity or individuality for him in ten years"; she "merely symbolized the job in the bank of which he had been deprived before he ever got it" (*The Sound and the Fury*, p. 321). Believing Quentin to be the living representation of his lost inheritance, Jason feels no compunction in depriving her of hers. Flem's treatment of Mink, on the other hand, goes unexplained. If he wished, he could easily have returned from his Texas honeymoon and with his influence and his money forced the waiving of the murder charge. Thus until the very last Bookwright insists to Ratliff that Flem will help his cousin: "Aint no man, I dont care if his name is Snopes, going to let his own blood kin rot in jail" (p. 325). It is interesting that in his desperate chase after his niece Jason unconsciously identifies himself with Milton's Satan and imagines himself dragging "Omnipotence

[68]

down from His throne, if necessary"; of tearing through
"the embattled legions of both hell and heaven" to get to
his fleeing niece (*The Sound and the Fury*, p. 322). It is
Jason who, in his desperation, fancies that he is capable of
such an encounter, but it is Flem who makes the journey
to the underworld and not only confronts the Prince of
Darkness but outsmarts him as well, at least as Ratliff imagines it.

Although the product of Ratliff's fantasizing imagination,
Flem's encounter with the Prince of Darkness places his
actions in a certain perspective so that whatever Flem does
is beyond the ordinary proportions of this world. Ratliff's
reverie follows Flem's usurpation of Frenchman's Bend in
which having once insinuated himself as Will Varner's
right-hand man, he then "like Abraham of old, [brought]
his blood and legal kin household by household, individual
by individual, into town, and established them where they
could gain money" (*Sartoris*, p. 172). The reverie itself is
directly brought on by Flem's marriage to Eula Varner and
Ratliff's subsequent recognition of the terrible waste involved in this act—"the beautiful masklike face" wed to
"the froglike creature barely reach[ing] her shoulder."
When Flem takes Eula away from Frenchman's Bend, he
takes with him, V. K. realizes, "the dream and wish of all
male under sun" (p. 149); it is an absence which brings on
that strange dry spell lasting throughout fall and winter too,
"without even a heatless wafer of sun to preside above a
dead earth cased in ice"—"from which the people as they
became older were to establish time and date events." As
has earlier been stated, it is Faulkner's own portrayal of the
myth of Persephone, and Flem's role in it is that of ravisher;
he becomes the sinister god of the underworld who snatches
Ceres's daughter away from the light and condemns the
earth to six months of barren desolation.

[69]

In his presentation of the scene in Hell Faulkner is deliberately drawing on similar scenes in epic and tragic literature. Flem's journey to the Underworld is evocative of Dante's *Inferno* and particularly of that passage of comic relief
in canto 22 where the sinner tricks the demons into allowing
him to escape the burning pitch by promising to bring
sinners of Italian birth to speak with Virgil and Dante. Like
Flem he is successful in duping the powers of the lower
world, and he leaves the demons in a condition of despairing
frustration not unlike that of Faulkner's Prince of Darkness
—aware that they have been bested, the "Evil-Talons"
argue with one another over the trickery and are left entan-
gled in their own pitch. There is, too, in Flem something
of Milton's Satan—this backwoods personification of evil
who, when offered Paradise, wants Hell. Throughout *The
Hamlet* Flem has been associated with fire. He is centrally
involved in the barn-burning affair—and to his threat of
arson Varner's only answer is a significant one: "He stopped
shouting because he stopped speaking because there was
nothing else to say, though it was going through his mind
fast enough: *Hell fire. Hell fire. Hell fire.*" (p. 21; italics
mine). There is also Labove's identification of Flem with
Vulcan, and the association is appropriate not only because
the god is the crippled consort of the supremely beautiful
Venus ("the beautiful masklike face" wed to "the froglike
creature"), but also because he is Hephaestus, the god of
fire. Like Milton's Satan, Flem is shrewdly able to judge the
particular weaknesses of human beings, and to use these
weaknesses to make them bring about their own downfall.
Thus the pattern of temptation and the fall repeats itself
in *The Hamlet.* There is Henry Armstid who because of his
simple greed for money, unredeemed by any higher motive,
is bested twice by Flem—once in the Texas auction and
again in the salting of the Old Frenchman's Place. He loses

his possessions and his sanity, digging "himself back into that earth which had produced him to be its born and fated thrall forever until he died" (p. 366), while his wife stands helplessly by like some tragic figure out of a Greek frieze—in "the gray garment hanging in rigid, almost formal folds like drapery in bronze" (p. 320). It is true, as one inhabitant of the Bend states, that perhaps "anybody might have fooled Henry Armstid," but Flem shows the extent of his power when he bests a much more formidable opponent, and one who is unwilling to bare his backside to the Snopeses. In the salting of the Frenchman's Place he beats not only Armstid, but V. K. too, and this same Yoknapatawphian continues his commentary on Henry's defeat: "Anybody might have fooled Henry Armstid. But couldn't nobody but Flem Snopes have fooled Ratliff" (p. 372).

The scene of Flem in Hell in which Faulkner's hill farmer makes a pact with the Devil over his soul and then wins the wager is perhaps most specifically evocative of the Faust legend. That Faulkner was most familiar with the legend is evidenced by the many times he alludes to it in his works. In *Absalom, Absalom!* Thomas Sutpen is compared by both Rosa and Shreve to Faust as a symbol of one who desires to go beyond ordinary human limitations; in the case of Sutpen this desire is manifested in his great ambition to create his design without benefit of the heritage or the tradition that lies behind such a concept. In *Light in August* Joe Christmas is identified with Faust in the scene at the dance in which he attempts to kill McEachern. The entire passage partakes of the atmosphere of Hell: the sweat of the horse is "sulphuric"; the "invisible wind flies past." In it Christmas "exults perhaps . . . as Faustus had, of having put behind [him] now at once and for all the Shalt Not, of being free at last of honor and law" (*Light in August*, p. 180). In his last work, *The Reivers*, Faulkner once again

[71]

turns to the Faust analogue in presenting the eleven-year-old Lucius Priest's first experience of "non-virtue" as he leaves boyhood behind to make his initiation trip into Memphis. "I was smarter than Boon," Lucius says. "I realized, felt suddenly that same exultant fever-flash which Faustus himself must have experienced: that of we two doomed and irrevocable, I was the leader, I was the boss, the master." And again, after experiencing the disillusionment that is part of growing up: "The exposing of the true shoddy worthlessness of the soul I had been vain enough to assume the devil would pay anything for" (*The Reivers*, pp. 53, 58).

The particular brilliance of the scene in Hell in *The Hamlet* lies in the fact that Faulkner does not simply allude to the Faust legend, but instead re-creates it, reshapes it according to his own imaginative genius. The figure who dares to enter Hades and challenge the Prince of Darkness over the redemption of his soul is never mentioned by name; instead he is identified by the asbestos ties he wears, the straw suitcase he carries, and the tobacco he unceasingly chews. While Goethe's Faust wants superhuman knowledge and therefore power ("to probe the hidden," he says), Flem is content with the earthly material power that wealth and the bank presidency can offer. Like Faust, Flem is tempted by the Devil. He is first offered the "gratifications," but the impotent Flem has no need to sell his soul for a Gretchen! He is next offered the "vanities," but Faulkner's Faust figure answers that the asbestos neckties he has brought along in his suitcase will do him just fine. In both Faulkner's and Goethe's versions of the Faust legend the Devil loses the wager. In Goethe, Faust regains his soul—"a great and matchless treasure"—through the power of love; in Faulkner the Prince cannot keep Flem's mortgaged soul because he can find no more trace of it than a smear in a matchbox. Upon discovering that they are the victims of the hoax, both Goethe's and Faulkner's princes exhibit similar behavior. In *Faust* the "Devils . . . fled in panic / . . . Even that old Satan-Master"; in *The Hamlet* Satan, "scrabbling across the floor, clawing and scrabbling" to get out of Hades and so away from Flem, offers him Paradise. While *Faust* ends with Faust's immortal soul being carried by angels into Heaven, Ratliff's reverie ends with Flem's refusal of Paradise and his desire, instead, for Hell. Part of the brilliance of Faulkner's presentation is that it is a parody of the Faust legend. The element of burlesque associated with parody, however, does not diminish Faulkner's portrayal of Flem as a force of evil. In the scene in Hell the Miltonic pattern of temptation and fall is repeated once again, and this time on a much grander scale. It is a case of the Tempter tempted, and in it Flem proves himself formidable enough to beat Satan at his own game.

In the last two books of the trilogy there is a profound change in Faulkner's presentation of Eula and Flem: the respective goddess and demon in *The Hamlet* have been reduced to ordinary size. In *The Town* Eula is still compared to Semiramis, Helen, Lilith, all in one, but it is not Faulkner now who uses these mythic allusions to describe her but his county attorney Gavin Stevens, who is hopelessly enamored of Flem Snopes's wife. Cleanth Brooks calls Eula the least romantic person in the novel (*The Yoknapatawpha Country*, p. 217). Gavin's long-winded oratory in which he romanticizes about an "earth . . . well lost for love, which . . . the weak and impotent and terrified and sleepless that the rest of the human race calls its poets, have dreamed and anguished and exulted and amazed over" is suddenly interrupted by the listening Eula. Not only does Eula speak in *The Town*, but hers is the voice of commonsense; the inert bucolic Venus has been replaced by a figure of practical intelligence: "You dont know very much about women, do

[73]

you?" she says. "Women aren't interested in poets' dreams.
They are interested in facts" (p. 226). Like Eula, Flem
Snopes in *The Town* and in *The Mansion* suffers a similar
reduction in size; the demonic personification of evil has
become, as Brooks suggests, "humanly wicked" (*The Yoknapatawpha Country*, p. 214). The Prince of Darkness can
and should inspire fear and revulsion, but never sympathy.
Accordingly, when Eula tells Gavin in *The Town* that Flem
is impotent, she adds: "You've got to be careful or you'll
have to pity him" (p. 331). Faulkner, in his remarks at
Charlottesville, indicates that he himself was disappointed
when Flem, in the later novels, yearned after respectability,
for it indicated that he was humanly motivated and this
weakened his effectiveness as a force of pure evil: "[I ad-
mired him] until he was bitten by the bug to be respectable,
and then he let me down." "The rapacious people—if
they're not careful—are seduced away and decide that what
they've got to have is respectability, which destroys one,
almost anybody. That is, nobody seems to be brave enough
anymore to be an out-and-out blackguard or rascal, that
sooner or later he's got to be respectable, and that finishes
it" (*Faulkner in the University*, pp. 33, 32). Brooks believes
that Faulkner's trimming down of Eula and Flem to normal
size is the result of his bringing them out of the brooding
countryside of *The Hamlet* into a small town, where they
are "compelled to breathe the air of a cozy world of little
rivalries and social feuds, scandals and church suppers, jokes
and cheerful gossip such as pervade any small town" (*The
Yoknapatawpha Country*, p. 193). The point, however, is
that this diminution does not negate their earlier presentation as figures larger than life; rather it serves to emphasize,
by contrast, that special aura of the supernatural and superhuman which surrounded Eula and Flem in *The Hamlet*,
where goddess and demon out of a more heroic time and

an older literature once again walk the "brooding country-side" of Frenchman's Bend.

Harry Levin suggests that "the characteristic point of view of American fiction" may very well be that which is represented by Isaac McCaslin in *Go Down, Moses*—of the boy who takes the major journey from innocence to experience —and he cites the heroes of Melville and Twain, Crane's *Red Badge of Courage*, and the stories of Hemingway.[3] When at the age of sixteen Ike leafs through the yellow pages of the family ledgers, whose entries, transcribed first by his grandfather and then by his father and uncle, record the acts of McCaslin injustice and cruelty, he discovers the sin of his heritage. In an effort to atone for his family Ike calls upon his experience in the wilderness, where in learning to be a hunter he also learned from Sam and old Ben the primitive virtues of courage and humility, endurance and compassion and sacrifice. Isaac McCaslin's personal quest for moral expiation is defined by Faulkner in mythological proportions. By his inclusion of the fourth section of "The Bear" (which is published only in *Go Down, Moses*), in which Ike summarizes all of American and world history from the Creation onward, Faulkner juxtaposes his young protagonist's initiation into manhood against the framework of the history of the human race, as it is presented from that particular religious perspective of the Book of Genesis. Ike's participation in the timeless world of the wilderness, a world of pristine innocence which antedates experience—where "only Sam and Old Ben and the mongrel Lion were taintless and incorruptible" (p. 191)—and his subsequent discovery of the McCaslin sin and its curse are to be viewed in terms of man's fall and expulsion from Paradise. *Go Down, Moses* is Faulkner's imaginative retelling of the Adamic myth, re-enacted now on the North American continent, in the

[75]

riter's own "little postage stamp of native soil," Yok-
apatawpha County.

The concept of an Edenic state of innocence and the
subsequent fall from this existence is that pattern which
unifies the individual stories in *Go Down, Moses*. The title
of "Was" establishes the story in time, and therefore in the
fallen world. It provides a historical perspective. The year
is 1859; the place is Faulkner's fictional Mississippi county,
and thus it is that period in history in which the Negroes
are held in bondage like the Israelites of old. But the story
is essentially comic, and as we learn later in "The Bear"
Buck and Buddy perpetuate old Carothers' sin of slavery
only to that degree of locking their slaves each night in the
big shell of a house "which lacked half its windows and had
no hinged back door at all." In the marvelous chase after
Tomey's Turl all ends well, but it prepares us for the more
tragic one in "The Bear." Like "Was" "The Fire and the
Hearth" is, on the whole, comic, but it contains a minor
plot which is, as James M. Mellard points out, "tragic in
its theme of loss of innocence and symbolic expulsion from
a youthful paradise."[4] This is that forty-five-year flashback
in which Lucas Beauchamp defies Zack Edmonds's ordering
Molly into the "big house" to care for Roth. At the demand
Lucas imagines himself crossing "a kind of Lethe"
—"emerging, being permitted to escape, buying as the price
of life a world outwardly the same yet subtly and irrevocably
altered" (p. 46). It is Lucas's rebirth into the world of experience, the same spiritual journey which the seven-year-old
Roth himself makes when he discovers that Lucas's son
Henry is "different" because he is black. It is a knowledge
which destroys their friendship: "So he [Roth Edmonds]
entered his heritage. He ate its bitter fruit" (p. 114). The
image is an evocation of both the fatal apple and the concept
of Original Sin, which in the case of the McCaslin family

[76]

is essentially a southern one, originating at that instant in
which old Carothers ordered his black daughter into his bed
because she was his property, and which is passed on, like
Adam's sin, to each succeeding generation: "The old curse
of his fathers, the old haughty ancestral pride based not on
any value but on an accident of geography, stemmed not
from courage and honor but from wrong and shame"
(p. 111).

In "The Old People" the twelve-year-old Isaac McCaslin
is baptized by Sam Fathers with the blood of the first buck
he has killed. At that moment Ike "ceased to be a child and
became a hunter and a man"—"forever one with the wilderness" (p. 178). It is an initiation into an idyllic realm—Eden
before the Fall—which is outside of time and hence without
death. Thus the ghost of that very buck which Ike has killed
can appear again—"full and wild and unafraid" (p. 184).
The title itself, "The Old People," alludes to a golden age
out of the past; theirs is a moral position prior to experience
which is preserved in the primitive virtues of the part Negro,
part Chickasaw chief and passed on to Ike. And so when
Sam tells his pupil about the old times, "Gradually to the
boy those old times would cease to be old times and would
become a part of the boy's present . . . the men who walked
through them actually walking in breath and air and casting
an actual shadow on the earth they had not quitted"
(p. 171). If "The Old People" portrays the prelapsarian state
of innocence, "Delta Autumn" portrays the postlapsarian
world after the Fall. In it Eden as both idyllic wilderness
and state of pristine innocence has been destroyed by Roth
Edmonds (and men like him), who perpetuates old Carothers McCaslin's original sin by committing incest with the
granddaughter of Tennie's Jim. The right attitude toward
man and the right attitude toward nature are indistinguishable, and so it is fitting that the deer Roth kills is not a buck,

but a doe. "No wonder the ruined woods I used to know dont cry for retribution," Ike realizes as he contemplates the land *"which man has deswamped and denuded and derivered in two generations. . . .* The people who have destroyed it will accomplish its revenge" (p. 364). In the final story, "Go Down, Moses," Roth evicts Samuel Worsham Beauchamp (yet another victim of old Carothers' original sin) from his plantation for petty thievery and is thereby indirectly responsible for Beauchamp's involvement with Chicago criminals and his subsequent execution as a murderer. Once again the situation is constructed in bibilical terms—"Roth Edmonds sold my Benjamin," Molly laments. "Sold him in Egypt. Pharaoh got him——" (p. 371).

By far the most important story in *Go Down, Moses,* in terms of statement of theme and scope of design, is "The Bear," and unlike the other stories which more or less follow a straightforward line of narration "The Bear" is not arranged according to chronological sequence. The first three sections present Ike's tutelage under Sam in the wilderness and end with Ben's death when Ike is sixteen; in section 4 Ike is twenty-one; but here, too, is the crucial flashback five years earlier when Ike discovers the sins of his heritage by looking through the family ledgers; in the fifth and final section Ike is eighteen when he returns once again to the hunting camp after it has been sold to the lumber company and he witnesses the beginning of the end of the wilderness after the deaths of Sam and old Ben. While "The Bear" is an apprenticeship story, it does not follow the chronological development of the protagonist who is initiated into manhood. Viewed in terms of the Adamic myth, however, it does follow the sequence of man's fall and expulsion from Paradise: first the presentation of the wilderness, the prelapsarian state; next the Fall itself when Ike gains from the

[78]

ledgers the knowledge of old Carothers' "original sin" and the curse he passes on to each succeeding generation; finally the expulsion into the postlapsarian world when Ike returns to the woods to see the beginning of the devastation that will be completed in "Delta Autumn"—where "the woods and fields [man] ravages and the game he devastates will be the consequence and signature of his crime and guilt, and his punishment" (p. 349).

"The Bear," like *Paradise Lost,* is no historical recapitulation of the book of Genesis. In *Go Down, Moses* Eden is conceived as a paradise of hunters. Thus in "Delta Autumn" the eighty-year-old Isaac McCaslin tells the hunting party gathered around the campsite that God created man and then created for him the kind of world that "He would have wanted to live in if He had been a man—the ground to walk on, the big woods, the trees and the water, and the game to live in it" (p. 348). By participating in the hunt—that "ancient and unremitting contest according to the ancient and immitigable rules which voided all regrets and brooked no quarter"—man comes as close to the state of perfect bliss as is possible on this earth: "the best game of all, the best of all breathing and forever the best of all listening." The hunt is a ritual of purification as well as a source of joy, and so the whiskey which the hunters drink is appropriately described as a religious libation; their conviviality around the campfire is at the same time a participation in the sacred rite of the Eucharist: "There was always a bottle present . . . those fine fierce instants of heart and brain and courage and wiliness and speed were concentrated and distilled into that brown liquor which not women, not boys and children, but only hunters drank, drinking not of the blood they spilled but some condensation of the wild immortal spirit, drinking it moderately, humbly even, not with the pagan's base and baseless hope of acquiring thereby the virtues of cunning and strength and speed but in salute to them" (p. 192).

One condition of Adam's Eden was that it was without change and therefore outside of time. Like Paradise Faulkner's wilderness antedates history—"the big woods, bigger and older than any recorded document" (p. 191). Old Ben, who at once is convincing as a real flesh and blood bear ("only Old Ben was an extra bear, the head bear General Compson called him") and as an embodiment of the spirit of the wilderness, possesses this same timeless quality which Eden possessed: "Not even a mortal beast but an anachronism indomitable and invincible out of an old dead time . . . epitome and apotheosis of the old wild life . . . the old bear, solitary, indomitable, and alone; widowered childless and absolved of mortality—old Priam reft of his old wife and outlived all his sons" (pp. 193–94). Because there was no time in Eden, there was no death either (both are consequences of Original Sin), and so Ike can place in the alcove above Sam's woodland grave the tobacco and peppermint candy his mentor used to love. Like Paradise before the Fall, the woods seem the wellspring of eternal life—"that place where dissolution itself was a seething turmoil of ejaculation tumescence conception and birth, and death did not even exist"[5] (p. 327). Thus it is fitting that Ike, after two years, can no longer find any trace of Sam and Lion's graves, since "the knoll . . . was no abode of the dead because there was no death, not Lion and not Sam: not held fast in earth but free in earth . . . and Old Ben too . . . they would give him his paw back even, certainly they would give him his paw back: then the long challenge and the long chase, no heart to be driven and outraged, no flesh to be mauled and bled" (pp. 328–29).

That state of pristine moral innocence which is a part of

Eden before the Fall is also associated with Faulkner's wilderness—a realm, unlike the "tamed land" against which it is juxtaposed, that is "of the men, not white nor black nor red but men, hunters, with the will and hardihood to endure and the humility and skill to survive" (p. 191). This "original innocence" is embodied in those three idealized figures who are so nearly a part of the nature around them that they die together on "the last day," that time which marks the beginning of the end of the Big Woods, "when even he [Ben] dont want it to last any longer" (p. 212). "Only Sam and Old Ben and the mongrel Lion," Faulkner says, "were taintless and incorruptible" (p. 191). From Lion, who is brave enough to challenge the giant bear and capable enough almost to succeed in the challenge, Isaac learns the quality of endurance—"the will and desire to endure beyond all imaginable limits of the flesh in order to overtake and slay" (p. 237). From the old bear with the trap-ruined foot he learns humility in order to become worthy of old Ben, "a sense of his own fragility and impotence against the timeless woods, yet without doubt or dread" (p. 200). He learns too from Ben the true meaning of freedom, a concept perverted by his grandfather at the instant that he summoned Eunice to his bed because she was his property—the wild and invincible old bear who loved freedom enough "to see it threatened not with fear nor even alarm but almost with joy" (p. 295). From his part Indian, part Negro tutor Ike learns "honor and pride and pity and justice and courage and love" (p. 297); later in his midnight conversation with his cousin McCaslin Edmonds he surmises it is what Keats meant by truth—"all things that touch the heart," and he appropriately thinks of Sam as Cass quotes from "Ode on a Grecian Urn." In slaying his first buck Ike also learns from Sam that he must be worthy of the life he takes: *"I slew you; my bearing must not shame your quitting life. My*

[81]

*conduct forever onward must become your death"* (p. 351).
It is an act which takes place in the wilderness before the
Fall and, in terms of the Adamic framework, in Paradise
before Cain murdered Abel; Ike's slaying of the buck is to
be seen in direct contrast to Roth's senseless killing of the
doe which takes place in "Delta Autumn," in the postlapsarian world.

When in "The Bear" Ike is initiated into the life of the
wilderness at the age of ten he is reborn in the true mystic
sense: "It seemed to him that at the age of ten he was
witnessing his own birth." The initiation is presented in
religious terms: Ike's apprenticeship in the woods becomes
a "novitiate . . . with Sam beside him" (p. 195). Like the
priest who forswears all earthly ties and with his vows takes
the church as his bride, God as his spiritual father and as
his mother the Virgin Mary, so Ike, in homage and tribute
to his experience in the wilderness, acknowledges his new
parentage: "Summer, and fall, and snow, and . . . spring
in their ordered immortal sequence, the deathless and im-
memorial phases of the mother who had shaped him if any
had toward the man he almost was, mother and father both
to the old man born of a Negro slave and a Chickasaw chief
who had been his spirit's father if any had, whom he had
revered and harkened to and loved and lost and grieved: and
he would marry someday . . . but still the woods would be
his mistress and his wife" (p. 326). After the initiation Ike
is reborn as an Adamic figure before the Fall. R.W.B. Lewis's description of the prelapsarian Adam also applies at this
moment to Isaac McCaslin: "His moral position was prior
to experience, and in his very newness he was fundamentally
innocent. The world and history lay all before him."[6] The
climax of Ike's initiation is his first encounter with old Ben.
In his personal quest to catch an actual glimpse of the fabled
bear, Isaac arms himself with a gun, a watch, and a compass.

As his exploration proceeds unrewarded, he voluntarily lays aside the gun. But this act is not enough; Ike "was still tainted." He continues to remain "alien and lost" in the wilderness until that point when "he relinquished completely to it" by giving up his watch and compass. These are those instruments which are evidence of man's civilization, symbolic of his scientific mastery of time and space. By liberating himself from time Ike can become one with the Edenic state, and in doing so he sees old Ben—he is able to experience his vision.

Section 4 is about history, the world in time and therefore after Eden. It is Faulkner's presentation of the Fall; structurally it follows immediately the portrayal of the untainted world of the wilderness, and it precedes the description of the devastation to the woods, begun in section 5 when they are sold to the lumber company and completed in "Delta Autumn" with Ike's expulsion from Paradise. The five generations of the white male line of McCaslins—old Lucius Quintus Carothers McCaslin, Uncle Buck and Uncle Buddy, Cass Edmonds, Isaac McCaslin, and Roth Edmonds —represent, in microcosm, all southern history in its sin and guilt and anguish; the ledgers which record the family's heritage become "that chronicle which was a whole land in miniature, which multiplied and compounded was the entire South" (p. 293). Ike's—and Faulkner's—interpretation of the history of the McCaslin family and, by extension, the history of the South is biblical.[7] In the midnight dialogue with his cousin Cass—"juxtaposed not against the wilderness but against the tamed land which was to have been his heritage" (p. 254)—Isaac sets in opposition to the McCaslin ledgers the Bible, the one book whose transcribers attempt to "write down the heart's truth" (p. 261). In God's covenant with man at the Creation, man is ordained to be overseer of the land, for all brotherhood to enjoy: "The earth is Jehovah's" (Exodus 9.29; Psalms 24.1; I Corinthians 10.26); "The earth hath he given to the children of men" (Psalms 115.16); "The land shall not be sold forever" (Leviticus 25.23).[8] This same covenant which God made with Adam Ike cites to Cass as reason for relinquishing his ownership of the McCaslin land: "He made the earth first and peopled it with dumb creatures, and then He created man . . . to hold suzerainty over the earth and the animals on it in His name, not to hold for himself and his descendants inviolable title forever, generation after generation . . . but to hold the earth mutual and intact in the communal anonymity of brotherhood, and all the fee He asked was pity and humility and sufferance and endurance and the sweat of his face for bread" (p. 257).

In the Adamic myth there was a fall and there had been a sin. In Faulkner the sin is the evil of slavery, which is rooted in the fault of pride and manifested in the lust for possession. It is epitomized by old Carothers' ordering first Eunice and then later Tomasina, the daughter he begot on Eunice, to his bed because they were his slaves—"that evil and unregenerate old man who could summon, because she was his property, a human being because she was old enough and female, to his widower's house and get a child on her and then dismiss her because she was of an inferior race" (p. 294). In the degree of its odiousness the act, which is performed by the progenitor of the line, becomes the McCaslins' original sin; when Ike comes to its entry in the ledger, he pronounces it to be "the specific tragedy which had not been condoned and could never be amortized" (p. 266). Like Adam's Original Sin the consequence of old Carothers' heinous crime is death. Six months before her daughter gives birth to her own father's child, Eunice drowns herself in the creek. The suicide elicits from Ike an unbelieving horror: *His own daughter His own daughter.*

[84]

*No No Not even him"* (p. 270). And like Adam's sin the original crime is perpetrated over and over by the succeeding generations—by the white male line of inheritors from old Carothers on the Negro line stemming from his miscegenation. In "The Fire and the Hearth" Zack Edmonds summons Molly Beauchamp because she is black to the "big house" to care for Roth and to satisfy his own desire; and when in "Delta Autumn" Roth Edmonds, named, appropriately enough, for old Carothers, uses in a similar way the granddaughter of Tennie's Jim, the old biblical notion of the sins of the father comes full circle.

In *Paradise Lost* Milton presents history as a providential pattern. This is that same view of history presented in *Go Down, Moses;* it is opposed to the objective theory of history, which records facts without finding in them any providential or moral pattern. In their midnight conversation Ike and Cass both conceive of history as succeeding eras of dispossession: "Dispossessed of Eden. Dispossessed of Canaan, and those who dispossessed him . . . dispossessed, and the five hundred years of absentee landlords in the Roman bagnios" and down through Columbus until old Carothers dispossessed Ikkemotubbe of the wilderness (pp. 258–59). The central act of dispossession in "The Bear" is the South's bondage of the Negro which is placed against the biblical context of the Israelites' being held in slavery by the Egyptians, an analogue supported both by the book's title and specifically by the expression of the situation in "Go Down, Moses" as a parallel to the Book of Exodus: "Roth Edmonds sold my Benjamin. Sold him in Egypt. Pharaoh got him——." When the angel Michael, in the eleventh book of *Paradise Lost,* allows Adam a foreknowledge of history, the first vision of human history given him is the slaying of Abel by Cain. This is the primal murder, the epitome of man's inhumanity to man which will be reenacted through-

[85]

out all the long ages. The murder has its counterpart in "The Bear," in Eunice's suicide for which old Carothers is indirectly responsible. It is this act which brings about God's curse on the McCaslin family. Like Adam's it is passed on to each succeeding generation though they had not participated in the primal sin—and appropriately enough it is presented in biblical terms: Ike "had inherited [the curse] as Noah's grandchildren had inherited the Flood although they had not been there to see the deluge" (p. 289).

When Michael in *Paradise Lost* permits Adam to see the vision of the Flood, destroying all but one family, Adam's initial response is one of horror. But once the archangel explains the reason for the Flood—that God's concern is not with numbers but with virtue—Adam utters an affirmation; he rejoices for that one man so perfect and so just that God created another world for him. In "The Bear" there is a strikingly parallel situation. It occurs at that point in Ike's recapitulation of the history of man when God, frustrated at the repeated acts of outrage and injustice against liberty and freedom, is about to repudiate His creation: "Not only that old world from which He had rescued them but this new one too which He had revealed and led them to as a sanctuary and refuge were become the same worthless tideless rock cooling in the last crimson evening." What prevents God's final destruction of the world He had made is Faulkner's Noah figure, John Brown, "one simple enough to believe that horror and outrage were first and last simply horror and outrage and was crude enough to act on that," who wins God's admiration when he utters what Moses, in a different context, might have thought: *"I am just against the weak because they are niggers being held in bondage by the strong just because they are white."* And so God turns back in hope "once more to this land which He still intended to save because He had done so much for it"—"with

[86]

woods for game and streams for fish and deep rich soil for seed and lush springs to sprout it and long summers to mature it and serene falls to harvest it and short mild winters for men and animals" (pp. 283–85).

What C. Vann Woodward says about America in general applies in section 4 specifically to the South, presented in "The Bear" as Canaan, or the Promised Land: "America was 'God's American Israel,' called out of a wicked and corrupt Old World and set apart by providence to create a new humanity and restore man's lost innocence."[9] It remains for Ike to explain to Cass why God would bring down on that section of the country He loves so well the devastation of the Civil War. Ike's justification of the catastrophe is the same as Milton's justification of the Flood. it is to save mankind and not destroy it, that out of His deep respect for John Brown's concrete act God will create another world for him. In both instances it is a tragic view of salvation: *Apparently they can learn nothing save through suffering,"* Ike imagines God saying, *"remember nothing save when underlined in blood"* (p. 286).

Section 4 ends with the scene in the bedroom in which Ike's wife promises him one night of complete sexual fulfillment. The concept of the physical expression of love becomes, here, a wager with high stakes in the balance—the night in exchange for the farm. If at this time she should become pregnant with Ike's son and thereby present him with an heir to the McCaslin inheritance, he will in turn agree to give up his idea of relinquishing the family plantation, an act which, to Ike, would absolve him from the pattern of McCaslin sin and guilt and punishment. Cleanth Brooks is too sympathetic with Faulkner's presentation of Isaac's wife when he agrees with Andrew Lytle that she acts as she does "for the sake of a communion of real marriage."[10] Faulkner himself calls her a prostitute, and goes

[87]

on to say that she used her sexuality in the hope of becoming the chatelaine of a plantation (*Faulkner in the University,* p. 275). In the bedroom scene Ike's wife is presented as an Eve figure, not so much as she is portrayed in Genesis, but more as Milton conceived of Adam's consort. In *Paradise Lost* the immediate effect of their eating the apple is the burning of the fires of passion in Adam and Eve, an anticipation of seduction in the fallen world. Ike's wife at the moment she offers him her body becomes the "composite of all woman-flesh since man that ever of its own will reclined on its back." Milton presents Eve—as well as Satan—in the role of tempter, and accordingly he has Adam taste the fatal apple not because he falls prey to the snake's enticement but out of his love for Eve; if she is expelled from Eden he will be also, for without her the Garden would no longer be Paradise. Faulkner's Eve is just as effective in her temptation of Isaac. He willingly gives in to her allure, and as he approaches her bed Ike evokes the original seduction and with it the memory of the original sin: "He said Yes and he thought, *She is lost. She was born lost. We were all born lost*" (p. 314).

This one night of passion, however, does not get for Ike the son to inherit the family estate, and so he relinquishes his ownership of the McCaslin plantation. Ike's sacrifice of the land is presented in biblical terms—as a contemporary parallel to Abraham's sacrifice of Isaac, that act in the Old Testament which epitomizes the Hebrew's humble spiritual surrender to God's will. When he renounces the plantation—"that whole edifice intricate and complex and founded upon injustice and erected by ruthless rapacity and carried on even yet with at times downright savagery" (p. 298)—Ike seeks to atone for old Carothers' perversion of God's covenant with Abraham: that he and his seed will receive all the land of Canaan "for an everlasting posses-

sion" (Genesis 17.8). Ike sees the analogy between himself
and the biblical Isaac, and in his conversation with Cass he
imagines God viewing him (who was born when Buck was
nearing seventy) as "an Isaac born into a later life than
Abraham's." While both Isaacs are sacrificial figures, Faulkner's protagonist, unlike his biblical namesake, does not
sacrifice himself for God, as Walter Brylowski points out,
but instead uses the land as a substitute.[11] So Ike continues
to compare himself with the biblical Isaac: "an Isaac born
into a later life than Abraham's," he tells Cass, and then
he adds significantly—"and repudiating immolation"
(p. 283).

In this inability to give of himself completely Ike is finally
incapable of the heroic act. His quest for salvation has all
along been a personal one; he cannot go the step further
and become an effective tool for the salvation of others. It
is a shortcoming compounded by the fact that Isaac consid-
ers himself to be one of God's elect: "Maybe He chose
Grandfather out of all of them He might have picked," Ike
tells Cass. "Maybe He knew that Grandfather himself
would not serve His purpose because Grandfather was born
too soon too, but that Grandfather would have descendants,
the right descendants . . . to set at least some of His lowly
people free" (p. 259). When Ike pronounces with pride that
"Sam Fathers set me free" (p. 300), he is talking about a
liberation from the McCaslin sin and, with it, a liberation
from the guilt and punishment of his heritage. Cass, however, sees the statement for what it really is—a renunciation
by Ike of the Mosaic role—and his reply constitutes a repri-
mand of his cousin's position which is not without justification: "You will be free—No, not now nor ever, we from
them nor they from us" (p. 299). In view of Ike's attitude
we can appreciate the full irony of that earlier scene in
which he confronts Fonsiba's husband, reading in his lens-

less, gold-framed spectacles—juxtaposed against "the empty fields without plow or seed to work them, fenceless against the stock which did not exist within or without the walled stable which likewise was not there"—enjoying in sloth Lincoln's emancipation. Recognizing the outrage which the black minister has committed against the concept of liberty, Ike cries out, "Freedom from what? From work? Canaan?" (p. 279). While Ike can see that in the case of Fonsiba's husband it is *"necessary for a man to distinguish between liberty and licence"* (pp. 289–90), he is unable to see how this distinction applies to his own life. When he says that Sam Fathers set him free, Isaac McCaslin is echoing the attitude of many young protagonists of initiation novels— Huck Finn, Eugene Gant, Stephen Dedalus—that freedom of the self is freedom from worldly responsibility.

When at the age of twenty-one Isaac becomes a carpenter, he does so in emulation of the archetypal figure of sacrifice: "Because if the Nazarene had found carpentering good for the life and ends He had assumed and elected to serve, it would be all right too for Isaac McCaslin" (p. 309). Ike imitates not so much the historical figure of Christ—a man always in the midst of other men, who suffered not for himself alone but so that others might be saved—as he does his own concept of Jesus as a man who, in order to renounce the Devil, felt he must also renounce the world. Thus Ike lives out his life—alone, continuing to live near the diminishing woods, making the "yearly pageant-rite" into the wilderness for two weeks each November where he tries to pass on to others the wisdom he learned from Sam but, as we discover in "Delta Autumn," without his old tutor's effectiveness. In terms of the Adamic framework Isaac's flaw is that he remains in the postlapsarian world an Adam *before* the Fall. As Richard P. Adams points out, Ike, by relinquishing the land, refuses to "till the ground," which was the means of Adam's salvation after eating the apple. An ascetic wed only to the wilderness, Ike is an Adam without any sons, and in his childless state he fails God's command: "Be fruitful and multiply" (Genesis 1.28).[12]

In terms of moral failure Isaac stops short of the paradox of the "fortunate Fall." The unfallen Adam's innocence was an innocence bred of ignorance; he was without the vast knowledge accumulated through experience. In the paradox of the fortunate Fall, in order to attain manhood, the individual had to fall, had to pass beyond childhood in an encounter with Evil[13]—for only by knowing evil could he recognize good and thereby make a significant choice between the two. In sections 4 and 5 of "The Bear" Ike is brought out of the timeless Edenic world of the wilderness and placed in history. Like Adam "who is at home only in the presence of Nature and God," he is thrust, as R.W.B. Lewis says, by circumstances "into an actual world and an actual age" (*The American Adam*, p. 89). It is here that Ike has the necessary encounter with evil when in looking through the ledgers he discovers old Carothers' primal sin. This is the moment of Ike's fall and therefore his opportunity for moral growth. But as we have seen, Ike abjures the role of a Moses, and he turns instead back to the wilderness in the hope of recapturing some part of his lost original innocence. Ike's retreat represents his repudiation of the actual world, the world in time, in favor of the cloistered and cloistering state of Paradise. To Faulkner such a retreat is a negative action, as he himself stated: "I don't hold to the idea of a return [to Nature]. That once the advancement stops then it dies. . . . We mustn't go back to a condition, an idyllic condition, in which the dream [made us think] we were happy, we were free of trouble and sin. We must take the trouble and sin along with us, and we must cure that trouble and sin as we go."[14] Because Ike operates effectively only in the woods, and hence outside of time, it is appropriate that in *Go Down, Moses* nothing happens to him between his twenty-first and eightieth year. There is a similar justification, too, in Roth's cruel remark in "Delta Autumn": "Where have you been all the time you were dead?" (p. 345).

In the fifth and final section of "The Bear" eighteen-year-old Isaac McCaslin returns to the wilderness for the first time since the deaths of Sam and old Ben two years earlier. The return is described as a homecoming; and, as Lewis perceives, "homecoming is for the exile, the prodigal son, Adam after the expulsion, not for the new unfallen Adam in the western garden" (*The American Adam*, p. 50). Ike's entry is thus appropriately marked by his encounter with the rattlesnake. It is an encounter with *the* original snake of Eden, an identification supported by Faulkner himself when he called the snake in section 5 the "old fallen angel":[15] "the old one, the ancient and accursed about the earth, fatal and solitary and he could smell it now: the thin sick smell of rotting cucumbers and something else which had no name, evocative of all knowledge and an old weariness and of pariah-hood and of death" (p. 329). Ike speaks to the snake in the same Indian tongue which Sam had used on that day six years before when he baptized his pupil in the blood of the first buck Isaac killed: "Chief," Ike said. "Grandfather." This scene is to be viewed against the earlier one in which Sam, by saluting the buck as "Grandfather," affirms that the same wild, free—and untainted—blood runs in them both (p. 350). Ike, however, addresses not the buck, but the snake in this expression of kinship, and by doing so he acknowledges his inheritance of original sin.

When Ike returns to the wilderness in section 5 he returns not to the Edenic realm which he had earlier known, but to the postlapsarian world. That there had been a fall is evidenced by his encounter with the snake, evocative of original sin and the expulsion from Eden; by the presence of death (Sam, old Ben, and Lion—the three "taintless and incorruptible" figures who were one with the wilderness —are all dead); by the presence of the railroad which, in cutting down the trees for the lumber company, devastates the big woods—whose prototype is significantly the old fallen snake of Eden: Ike "watched the train's head . . . vanish into the wilderness, dragging its length of train behind it so that it resembled a small dingy harmless snake vanishing into weeds" (p. 318); and by that strange and puzzling scene with Boon and the squirrels which ends "The Bear." After his encounter with the rattlesnake Ike crosses the clearing and comes to the gum tree where he was to meet Boon. There he sees forty or fifty frantic squirrels, leaping and darting from branch to branch "until the whole tree had become one green maelstrom of mad leaves"; at the base of the trunk a hysterical Boon, sitting with his back against the tree, is furiously hammering one piece of his dismantled gun with another piece in "the frantic abandon of a madman" (p. 331). Boon and the isolated gum tree are located precisely at the dividing line between the deforested land of "civilized" life where Ike gained the knowledge of his heredity and the primitive forest where he was initiated into an unspoiled Edenic realm in which a kind of original innocence was once again possible.[16] The scene itself is juxtaposed against the earlier one in which Boon successfully kills old Ben; it emphasizes, through its reduction, the "heroic tragedy of the bear and the dog," as Faulkner himself has said: "To me it underlined the heroic tragedy of the bear and the dog by the last survivor being reduced to the sort of petty comedy of someone trying to patch up a gun in order to shoot a squirrel" (*Faulkner in the University*, p. 60). In the chase after old Ben, the object of the hunt possesses a mythic stature: "Not even a mortal beast but an anachronism indomitable and invincible out of an old dead time." Boon's killing of Ben, moreover, is a heroic act. He kills the bear not with a gun—which he now uses to hunt the squirrels and which, as we have learned from Ike's quest when he saw the celebrated bear for the first time, is a tainted weapon—but with the primitive woodsman's knife, and thereby in the manner of a sacrificial rite. In his "loverlike" clasp of old Ben, Boon expresses through gesture that reverential attitude which Ike says a hunter should have for the life he takes: *"I slew you; my bearing must not shame your quitting life. My conduct forever onward must become your death"* (p. 351). In the subsequent scene with Boon and the squirrels, prepared for by the entry of the snake into the wilderness which immediately precedes it, Isaac realizes that the heroic hunting age—symbol in "The Bear" of the prelapsarian Edenic state—has passed forever. Boon's frantic "Get out of here! Dont touch them! Dont touch a one of them! They're mine!" (p. 331) is a hysterical cry of possession; it is evocative of both old Carothers' original sin and the history of the human race since the Fall: "Dispossessed of Eden. Dispossessed of Canaan, and those who dispossessed him dispossessed."

Viewed at its most literal level, *As I Lay Dying* is the story of the efforts of a poor and ignorant hill family, the Bundrens, to bury Addie Bundren, the wife and mother, with her relatives in the cemetery at Jefferson and of the obstacles they encounter in this odyssey from Frenchman's Bend to their destination twenty miles away. The central and controlling image of the novel is the journey itself. Of the journey motif in general, Robert D. Jacobs says it is "the one universal story, the subject-matter of folklore and the clear allegory of every human life."[17] The very structure of the book calls forth echoes from out of myth and legend: the epic hero's journey to the land of the dead, the trek out of Egypt to the Promised Land, the medieval pilgrimage of the soul to salvation. In a deliberate evocation of these analogues Faulkner has succeeded in juxtaposing the actions of the Bundren family—sometimes foolish, even grotesque, at other times courageous to a superhuman degree—against the backdrop of a world of heroic ideals.

Elizabeth Kerr interprets *As I Lay Dying* to be formally patterned after the idealized quest of the old romances.[18] She sees Dewey Dell in the role of the distressed damsel, with Jewel as the hero of the myth who braves flood and fire to reach and rescue his beloved. In view of the Bundrens' selfish private motives in getting to Jefferson—which are opposed to the precious objects brought back from the traditional quest—Miss Kerr, however, is finally forced to conclude that *As I Lay Dying* is Faulkner's perversion of the medieval quest, and as such it is "incompatible with any sentimental or heroic concept"; rather, she says, "it is the essence of ironic mockery." In her argument Miss Kerr has touched on what is perhaps the central problem in approaching the novel—that in Faulkner's blending of the grotesque and the heroic (a blending which is both daring and ingenious), he has created a complexity of tone, which, as Cleanth Brooks says, "has proved difficult for some readers to cope with" (*The Yoknapatawpha Country*, p. 141). In *As I Lay Dying* there are presented not one but two distinct quests, and each has its own obstacles. The first is the funeral journey in which the family as a whole cooperates to bury Addie; it is presented as the fulfillment of an ethical obligation, since the family has promised their dying mother that they will bury her not in New Hope where the Bundrens are buried and which is only three miles away but with her own family in Jefferson, a twenty-mile trek. "I give

[95]

her my word," Anse says. "It is sacred on me. . . . She is counting on it" (*As I Lay Dying*, p. 438). What is a serious obligation to the Bundrens becomes to the detached neighbor Tull a foolish and unnecessary bother: "His [Anse's] folks buries at New Hope, too, not three miles away. But it's just like him to marry a woman born a day's hard ride away and have her die on him" (p. 357). But the Bundrens persevere; they successfully complete the nine-day journey to Jefferson, even when, during its course, they are called on to contend with the ancient catastrophes of fire and flood.

There are, at the same time, the individual quests by those members of the Bundren household who set out for Jefferson in the pursuit of more private motives. Approaching the bed of his wife at the moment after her death, Anse touches her face and hands, then clumsily tries to smooth her quilt with his hand, "awkward as a claw," in a bumbling gesture of feeling—and then: "God's will be done," he says. "Now I can get them teeth" (p. 375). Dewey Dell grieves at her mother's death, but she is unable to mourn Addie properly because she is so obsessed with her own problem. Intuiting her desperate need for an abortion, Darl perceives his sister's reason for wanting to go to Jefferson: "You want her to die so you can get to town: is that it?" (p. 365). Unlike Anse and Dewey Dell, Vardaman shows real grief over Addie's death. However grotesque Vardaman's freeing of Peabody's team and his drilling the holes in his mother's coffin may seem, they are acts which nevertheless reveal the anguish of a small boy who has undergone a catastrophic experience. The grief, however, is not so terrible that it cannot be made more bearable by the anticipation of seeing the red train in the store window. Thus after witnessing Addie's burial and Darl's capture, Vardaman combines the train with the misfortune in one unbroken thought— *"Darl he went to Jackson is my brother Darl is my brother* Only it was over that way, shining on the track" (p. 524). W. P. Ker in his classic work, *Epic and Romance,* states that the presence of private motives in a heroic quest is not an uncommon characteristic of the ancient epic: "There often appears a contradiction between between the story of individual heroes, pursuing their own fortunes, and the idea of a common cause to which their own fortunes ought to be, but are not always, subordinate."[19] Ker cites as example the *Chanson de Roland,* in which Roland's pride and self-reliance—manifested in his refusal to sound the horn at the battle of Roncesvalles—led to disaster. In *As I Lay Dying* the inclusion of the Bundrens' private motives for making the odyssey to Jefferson does not pervert, as Elizabeth Kerr maintains, the concept of the idealized quest (and it is even justified by the old epic conventions, as these are presented by W. P. Ker). Instead it has to do with Faulkner's skillful and inventive blending of heroism and farce without destroying the heroic; it is what Olga Vickery points to when she calls the novel a success, only she characterizes it as "two modes of response to the same set of characters and events" (*Novels,* p. 65). This successful mingling is perhaps best summed up by Tull, at that moment just before the Bundrens are to undergo their trial by the flood: "Just going to town. Bent on it." And then he goes on to prophesy: "They would risk the fire and the earth and the water and all just to eat a sack of bananas" (p. 438).

Faulkner associates with the Bundrens (and especially with their nine-day odyssey) images from the book of Revelation which describe the Apocalypse, and in doing so he makes the trek which his ignorant tenant farmers take from Frenchman's Bend to Jefferson into a marvelous journey beyond ordinary time and space.[20] Six times before Addie's death he uses the adjective *sulphurous* to describe either the

Bundrens or their surroundings and thereby gives to the death scene a quality shared with Hades. The first instance occurs in Darl's section when he mysteriously predicts to Jewel that Addie Bundren will die: "The sun, an hour above the horizon, is poised like a bloody egg upon a crest of thunderheads; the light has turned copper: in the eye portentous, in the nose sulphurous, smelling of lightning" (p. 366). The whole passage seems to foretell an end of things; it is especially evocative of the sixth chapter of Revelation: "And I beheld when he had opened the sixth seal, and, lo, there was a great earthquake; and the sun became black as sackcloth of hair, and the moon became as blood." The second instance is in the scene in which Darl imagines the Falstaffian figure of Dr. Peabody being hauled up the mountainside by rope so that he might reach the Bundren house—thus Darl sees him going "balloon-like up the sulphurous air" (p. 366). In the third and fourth instances the Bundren farm is associated with sulphur: "There is a little daylight up here still, of the colour of sulphur matches. The boards look like strips of sulphur" (p. 368). The fifth time is that description of the "sulphur-coloured light" when Anse realizes that Addie's mind is set on dying (p. 369). In the sixth and final instance the adjective is used to describe the smell of the air at that moment when the rain begins; it is that instant which, as we will discover, is the beginning of the flood (p. 392).

The juxtaposition of the Bundren journey and the Apocalypse reaches a climax with the presentation of the flood waters which overturn Anse's wagon and destroy his team. The one dominant image at this point is the metaphor of chaos, which announces both the beginning and the end of Creation. Thus to Tull the bridge goes down "into the moiling water like it went clean through to the other side of the earth . . . and them that would walk up outen the water on that side must come from the bottom of the earth" (p. 435). And similarly to Darl: "Above the ceaseless surface they stand—trees, cane, vines—rootless, severed from the earth, spectral above a scene of immense yet circumscribed desolation filled with the voice of the waste and mournful water" (p. 439). Just as the Apocalypse foretells the end of the earth by fire ("The first angel sounded, and there followed hail and fire mingled with blood, and they were cast upon the earth: and the third part of trees was burnt up, and all green grass was burnt up"—Revelation 8.7), so there is something of the Doomsday description in the scene in which Darl sets fire to Gillespie's barn to put an end to the outrage of a corpse nine days dead and still unburied. "Overhead the flames sound like thunder" (p. 498), and when Vardaman looks up to see the barn engulfed in the fire what he sees for an instant is the elemental state of chaos: "Then [the barn] went swirling, making the stars run backward without falling" (p. 503).

The odyssey from Frenchman's Bend to Jefferson is specifically a funeral journey; and the wagon, the corpse, the coffin, and the buzzards constitute—albeit a bizarre one—a funeral procession. The image of the procession moving toward its final destination evokes the medieval soul's pilgrimage toward redemption and calls forth such works as the *Divine Comedy, Piers Plowman,* and *Pilgrim's Progress.* Like the Bundrens Dante, Langland's Will, and Bunyan's Christian all must overcome physical obstacles which hinder their allegorical journey to salvation. Specifically the straight and narrow path in *Pilgrim's Progress* which runs up hill and down again, through city and wilderness, to the Black River, terminating finally at the Shining Gate of Celestial City has a curious parallel in the flood-ruined road to Jefferson. Michael Millgate perceives in *As I Lay Dying* an echo of Bunyan's masterpiece, and he points to the Bundren family name as a possible phonetic allusion the burden which Christian carries on his journey to the Celestial City.[21] In his novel Faulkner does seem to be drawing on *Pilgrim's Progress*, but it is for the humor which results when his characters' actions are seen in the context of Bunyan's work. Anse, like Christian, does consider himself tested by God, but the divine burden around his neck is regarded by Faulkner's protagonist not as a necessary means to salvation, but more as a bother; it even becomes, at times, a perverse source of pride, as a measure of how much he, as a man, can stand. As he watches the rain pour down which will eventually flood the river, Anse believes he is singled out from every other man in Yoknapatawpha County to receive God's misfortune: "And now I can see same as second sight the rain shutting down betwixt us, a-coming up that road like a durn man, like it wasn't ere a other house to rain on in all the living land" (p. 364). Similarly, when he looks down at Cash who almost lost his life in his confrontation with the swollen river, Anse murmurs, "If ever was such a misfortunate man" (p. 457). At this moment, however, he is talking not about his son, but himself: " 'Fore God, if there were ere a man in the living world suffered the trials and floutings I have suffered" (p. 477). When Dewey Dell fails to get her abortion at the town of New Hope, Faulkner is "having at" Bunyan's allegorical nomenclature. Dewey Dell's "new hope" is entirely a worldly one, prompted in her case by the pressure of expediency; it has nothing at all to do with the Celestial City!

In the context of the purpose of their pilgrimage, the Bundrens' encounter with the flood waters calls to mind the River Styx, the river of death in pagan mythology across which Charon ferried the lost souls down to Hades. In biblical terms the river evokes the sacred waters of baptism and a rebirth, through this rite, into a new state of spiritual salvation. It evokes the River Jordan, presented as the eastern boundary of the Promised Land in the Old Testament and the site where Christ was baptized by John the Baptist in the New. As he does with *Pilgrim's Progress,* Faulkner is deliberately drawing on these analogues as a kind of archetypal framework against which to measure his characters' actions. We know, for example, that Addie does not believe in the spiritual, and in her attitude she is directly contrasted to Cora Tull and the Reverend Whitfield—both of whom pervert the Christian concept of salvation. Spouting her religious platitudes, Cora is an example of one who does the right thing for the wrong reason. It is true that she tries to give·the dying Addie companionship and therefore comfort, just as it is true that she tries to console Vardaman in his grief, but these acts are done apparently not so much for the sake of the Bundren family as they are to ensure her own entry into heaven. Thus Tull's observation about his wife has more than a little truth in it: "Now and then a fellow gets to thinking. About all the sorrow and afflictions in this world; how it's liable to strike anywhere, like lightning. I reckon it does take a powerful trust in the Lord to guard a fellow, though sometimes I think that Cora's a mite over-cautious, like she was trying to crowd the other folks away and get in closer than anybody else" (p. 388). The Reverend Whitfield is even less admirable than Cora, for he is unwilling to do the deed that will get him into heaven. Having fathered Addie's illegitimate son Jewel, Whitfield, upon learning that Addie is dying, sets out to admit his adultery to the wronged husband. However, when the preacher discovers that Addie has died without saying any word about the adultery, he makes no confession—at least not the one of consequence which would have been to Anse: "I have sinned, O Lord. . . . But He is merciful; He will accept the will for the deed, Who knew that when I framed the words of my confession it was to Anse I spoke them, even though he was not there" (p. 469). Whitfield's doctrine of accepting "the will for the deed" is a convenient one, for it enables the minister—who is not loath to see the Bundren farm as the scene of his Gethsemane (p. 469)—to attain an immediate "salvation" without suffering. It is a perversion of the concept of the Word, and one which enables Whitfield, at once both confessor and priest, to pronounce himself saved.

As Brooks points out, Addie's body is the symbol of her identity (*The Yoknapatawpha Country*, p. 149). Though the flood waters may call to mind the journey along the Styx or the rite of baptism, there is no spiritual rebirth for Addie Bundren.[22] After death her vital will appears still to live on in her body, so that her coffin seems to "slumber lightly alive, waiting to come awake" (p. 395). Thus when Vardaman bores the holes in his mother's coffin in order that she can breathe, it is to take care of Addie's physical needs. Finally it is the corpse itself which becomes the instrument of Addie's revenge, and Anse and the Bundren children gain no rest from their trials until they bury the decayed body— which along the trek to Jefferson has attracted the circling buzzards and protests from the outraged onlookers—in her family's cemetery. Just as Addie's body is the symbol of her identity, so her salvation is a physical one, and it is to be viewed—by contrast—against the medieval soul's pilgrimage to redemption. To Cora's act of praying for her soul, Addie's answer is a prophetic one: "Because people to whom sin is just a matter of words, to them salvation is just words too" (p. 468). Her salvation will not be of the soul, but of the body; and thus when she says, "He is my cross and he will be my salvation. He will save me from the water and from the fire. Even though I have laid down my life, he will save me" (p. 460), Addie is talking not about Christ and the River Jordan and the fires of hell, but of Jewel and his rescue of her corpse from the flood waters and from the fire of Gillespie's burning barn.

The Bundrens' nine-day journey suggests, in theme and structure, the journey of the Israelites from Egypt to the Promised Land. Addie's desire to be buried with her own family in the cemetery at Jefferson is echoed in Exodus 14.12 with the expression of the Israelites' fear that they will die in the wilderness and go unburied and again in Exodus 13.19 in which Moses in his trek takes with him the bones of Joseph so that he can be buried *with his people*. The climax of the book of Exodus is the passage over the Red Sea in which the Egyptians are drowned in the waters while the Israelites, God's chosen people, are allowed to walk safely across upon dry land after Moses, following the Lord's instruction, has parted the sea with his rod. The analogue in *As I Lay Dying* is, of course, the Bundrens' disastrous encounter with the flood waters. The drowning of the Egyptians "with their chariots and horsemen all swallowed up" is specifically paralleled by Cash's near-drowning and the total destruction of Anse's wagon and team. We learn from Darl that Anse was sick once from working in the sun when he was a young man, and he tells people that if he ever sweats he will die (p. 348). It is Anse's excuse for his own laziness, and it gives him a reason not to participate in the rescue when the river overflows. Thus he, like the Israelites, stays on dry land; he watches from his vantage point on the river bank Jewel's courageous efforts to save Cash. And, like the Israelites, Anse is portrayed as one of God's elect; "I reckon [the Lord] is like everybody else around here," Will Varner says. "He's done [taken care of Anse] so long now He can't quit" (p. 402). The analogue to Moses' rod "which turns the Red Sea to blood" is the log which crashes into the wagon and thereby causes the disaster which follows. It is presented as an act of divine intervention: "Log, fiddlesticks!," Cora says. "It was the hand of God." While we might question Cora's interpretation as one who sees the hand of God in just about everything, her husband is a more impartial witness: "They was going about it right and they would have made it if it hadn't a-been for that log. . . . Soon as the wagon got tilted good, to where the current could finish it, the log went on. It headed around the wagon and went on good as a swimming man could have done. It was like it had been sent there to do a job and done it and went on" (pp. 448–49).

After Moses delivers the Ten Commandments, he gives to the Israelites other laws which govern their civil obedience, one of which has a curious parallel in *As I Lay Dying:* "If fire break out . . . so that the field be consumed *therewith,* he that kindled the fire shall surely make restitution" (Exodus 22.6). God's judgment is borne out when Darl sets Gillespie's barn on fire in an effort to put an end to the outrage of the still unburied body. Darl indeed makes restitution for his action; he becomes the family sacrifice. He is violently jumped upon by Jewel and Dewey Dell out of fear and hatred that he knows their secrets—the illegitimacy of the one, the pregnancy of the other—and sent to Jackson —an act which the family sees as the only alternative to being sued by Gillespie (p. 509). Like the Israelites who survive their trials and are delivered into Canaan, "unto a land flowing with milk and honey," so the Bundrens arrive at their appointed destination. The cemetery at Jefferson is literally the promised land: "I give her my promised word in the presence of the Lord," Anse says. "It is sacred on me. . . . She is counting on it"(pp. 426, 438).

By remarks made at Charlottesville and by the title of the novel (which is probably taken from the eleventh book of the *Odyssey*), Faulkner indicates that he himself conceived of the Bundren procession to Jefferson in terms of the framework of the epic journey: "I simply imagined a group of people and subjected them to the simple universal natural catastrophes, which are flood and fire, with a simple natural motive to give direction to their progress."[23] In their trek to the cemetery at Jefferson the Bundrens make the epic hero's pilgrimage to the land of the dead and thereby evoke Ulysses in the eleventh book of the *Odyssey,* Aeneas in the sixth book of the *Aeneid,* and Dante. In *As I Lay Dying,* as in the ancient epic, supernatural forces—gods, angels, and demons—interest themselves in the action and intervene from time to time. Mention has already been made of the log, which in the flood scene is seen as an act of divine intervention. More than an instrument of God, the log appears to be a manifestation of the deity itself, and as such it calls to mind the old pagan gods' leaving the slopes of Olympus to mix in the affairs of mortals on earth. Darl compares the log to Christ, whose walking on the surface of the water is described by St. John: *"It surged up out of the water and stood for an instant upright upon that surging and heaving desolation like Christ"* (p. 445). Presented as a pagan as well as a Christian deity, the log—with the long streamer of foam hanging on one end of it "like the beard of an old man or a goat" (p. 445)—is metamorphosed and becomes the old god Pan. Finally, as in the epic, Faulkner's characters are made to undergo an ordeal of enormous difficulty, and some of the Bundrens, at least, emerge from their trials as heroic personalities, capable both of great deeds of courage and of great suffering.

Although in no sense of the word can Anse be described as heroic, he is remarkable in his ability to go through the trials to which the Bundren family is subjected and emerge untouched. Elizabeth Kerr in her *"As I Lay Dying* as Ironic Quest" sees Anse, in light of his magical powers over others —including, as we have learned from Will Varner, God

Himself—as a Merlin figure: "Be durn if there ain't something about a durn fellow like Anse that seems to make a man have to help him, even when he knows he'll be wanting to kick himself next minute," Tull says, not without a touch of admiration. "I be durn if Anse don't conjure a man, some way. I be durn if he ain't a sight" (pp. 480, 481). Anse replaces combat, the characteristic maneuver in epic, with stratagem.[24] While it is true that he does exhibit a certain amount of honor, as in his death vigil over Addie's coffin in Samson's barn or in his mortgage of his own cultivator and seeder so that he will not be "beholden" to Armstid who offers him the loan of his team, still Anse, afraid to sweat for fear he might die, relies on others to get him through the obstacles along the road to Jefferson—on Samson's and Armstid's and Gillespie's hospitality, on Dewey Dell's abortion money, on the eight dollars Cash had saved to buy a phonograph, and on Jewel's horse, though that horse was the only thing Jewel loved besides Addie. In the end it is not Addie but Anse who experiences a rebirth, albeit a worldly one; he walks away from his trial by flood and fire with new teeth, a new wife, and a new gramophone. Faulkner himself cites Anse as an example of one who successfully coped with his fate;[25] and in his marvelous capacity for survival—largely a result of his ability to make others suffer and sacrifice for him—Anse meets Daniel Hoffman's definition of the "folk protagonist": "The self-determinative hero," whose "powers prove the self spiritually indomitable and adaptable to the wildest vicissitudes of fortune and nature."[26]

On the journey to Jefferson, Darl represents, as Cleanth Brooks has pointed out, the "antiheroic intelligence" (*The Yoknapatawpha Country*, p. 145). Darl is almost pure perception. He exhibits remarkable powers of clairvoyance, divining the secret of Jewel's birth and intuiting Dewey Dell's

reason for coming to Jefferson. He also recognizes the outrage in the journey itself, that, as Faulkner himself has said,
the dragging around of the "dead putrefying body" was to
him "a violation of some concept, some shape of beauty"
(*Faulkner in the University*, p. 110). Significantly it is Darl
who compares the log, which crashes into the wagon and
thereby prevents the Bundrens from crossing the flood waters without mishap, to Christ. Unsuccessful in his attempts
to persuade his family to bury the decaying corpse as quickly
as possible, Darl assumes what he interprets to have been
the role of the log—that of stumbling block to the completion of the quest. Having told Vardaman that Addie "wants
[God] to hide her away from the sight of man" (p. 495),
he sets fire to Gillespie's barn in the hope of cremating his
mother's body. All along Darl has eschewed the heroic gesture. When, for example, the wagon is overturned in the
flooded river, Darl jumps free, relinquishing to Cash and
Jewel the role of deliverer. Later, when Tull tells Cora of
the event, she chides him about Darl's failure to participate
in the rescue: "And you're one of the folks that says Darl
is the queer one, the one that ain't bright, and him the only
one of them that had sense enough to get off that wagon.
I notice Anse was too smart to been on it a-tall" (p. 448).
However, as consequence of his setting the barn on fire,
Darl, alone of all the Bundrens, is called upon to make the
supreme sacrifice—himself: *"My Brother Darl,"* Vardaman
thinks, *"went crazy and went to Jackson both. Lots of people
didn't go crazy. Pa and Cash and Jewel and Dewey Dell and
me didn't go crazy. . . . We didn't go to Jackson either"*
(p. 525).

From their trials along the road to Jefferson two of the
Bundrens—Jewel and Cash—emerge as heroic figures, the
one through his deeds, the other through his suffering. Years
later at Charlottesville Faulkner pointed specifically to Jewel

as an example of a man trying to do better than he thought he could (*Faulkner in the University*, p. 109). Fulfilling the role designated for him in Addie's prophecy, it is Jewel who saves his mother's body from the flood and from the fire; he is the Bundren who most successfully confronts "the two greatest catastrophes man can suffer"—not with stratagem but with the old epic hero's gesture of combat. Having successfully dragged his mother's coffin out of the flooded river, he continues to dive back into the swollen waters —against the wise advice of Tull, who warns him to look out for his own safety—until he retrieves Cash's tools. His motive is simple—because the tools mean so much to his brother. Jewel rescues Addie's body from Gillespie's burning barn with that same furious intensity which he exhibited at the flood-swollen river. The scene (as has earlier been mentioned) is described in apocalyptic images, and Jewel braves "the flames overhead sound[ing] like thunder" to save first Gillespie's horse and cow and then "single-handedly" his mother's coffin, though he must fight off Darl and Dewey Dell and then Gillespie, who physically tries to restrain him from entering the barn once again, to do so. At the moment Jewel saves Addie "he appears to be enclosed in a thin nimbus of fire" (p. 501), and Richard Adams observes that it is a description evocative of the figure of Christ as he is portrayed in Byzantine mosaics (*Myth and Motion*, p. 75).

In a different sense Jewel's sacrifice of his horse is just as heroic as his saving of Addie's coffin from flood and fire. In the rescue attempts Jewel is operating instinctively; he is the man of almost pure action (only one section in the novel is allocated to Jewel's perspective of events as compared to Darl's nineteen), and his rushing in to save his mother's body—first from the river and then from the burning barn—is almost a reflex action. When he agrees to trade his horse to that Anse can buy another team and thereby continue the journey, he is giving up a part of himself. Jewel "sacrificed the only thing he loved for someone else's good," Faulkner said at Charlottesville. "This man who loved nothing but that horse would never have believed that he would have sacrificed that horse for anything, yet when the crisis came he did behave better than he thought he would behave" (*Faulkner in the University*, p. 109). Just how much this sacrifice means to Jewel is revealed in the flashback when Darl tells how his brother paid for the horse, laboring for five months to clear forty acres of Quick's land—doing it "single-handed, working at night by lantern"—and then sneaking home again at dawn to do his own chores in his father's field. "I have seen him go to sleep chopping," Darl says, "watched the hoe going slower and slower up and down, with less and less of an arc, until it stopped and he leaning on it motionless in the hot shimmer of the sun" (p. 429).

While Jewel is heroic to the extent that he exhibits how much a man can do, Cash is heroic in his demonstration of how much a man can stand. It is not so much Jewel—though it is true that Jewel is Addie Bundren's "salvation"—who, as Adams maintains, is a Christ figure, but rather it is Cash. Like Christ, Cash is a carpenter, and Dewey Dell watches him "sawing the long hot sad yellow days up into planks and nailing them to something" (p. 355). Isaac McCaslin is also a carpenter, but there is a significant difference here; unlike Cash, Ike deliberately takes up the trade in conscious emulation of Christ, and thus it is Isaac, and not Faulkner, who is calling up the analogue in "The Bear." Cash possesses many of the attributes which Jesus the man possessed—kindness, charity, and a measureless capacity to suffer for others. These are all quiet qualities that might easily go unnoticed, and indeed it is part of Cash's personality that he often remains a background figure. When, for example, the log crashes into the wagon and overturns the team, it is Cash who, even though he is unable to swim, holds on to Addie's coffin while Darl chooses to jump to safety. But shortly thereafter Cash is hurt, and his heroic gesture is subsequently overshadowed by Jewel's successful rescue. It is Cash, too, who, when he finds out why the fifteen-year-old Jewel is sneaking out of the house at night, quietly and without fanfare takes over part of Jewel's chores at home: "I would find him doing some of Jewel's work around the house," Darl says, "work that pa still thought Jewel was doing and that ma thought Dewey Dell was doing. So I said nothing to him, believing that when he got done . . . he would tell me. But he never did" (p. 432).

In his passive suffering Cash matches, in heroic capability, Jewel's ability to perform the courageous deed. When the wagon overturns in the river and Cash breaks his leg he endures the pain without complaint, just as he endures without complaint the agony of riding six days on a wagon without springs while the broiling sun and the homemade cast Anse has fashioned from sand and cement turn his broken leg black. "It never bothered me much," Cash tells Peabody, though Peabody notices sweat drops as "big as marbles running down his face and his face about the colour of blotting-paper" (p. 516). When Darl is sent to Jackson, only Cash shows any sympathy for his plight. Jumped on by Dewey Dell and Jewel, Darl knows to turn to his older brother as his only possible ally: "I thought you would have told me," Darl says, lying on his back and looking up at Cash. "I never thought you wouldn't have" (p. 514). Cash will even try to justify Darl's actions on the journey: "I thought more than once before we crossed the river and after, how it would be God's blessing if He did take her outen our hands and get shut of her in some clean way, and it seemed to me that when Jewel worked so to get her outen the river, he was going against God in a way, and then when Darl seen that it looked like one of us would have to do something, I can almost believe he done right in a way." Cash, however, is limited in his intellectual comprehension, and he concludes: "But I don't reckon nothing excuses setting fire to a man's barn and endangering his stock and destroying his property." And then unable to rid his mind of his brother's plight, he adds, "But it's a shame, in a way" (p. 510).

Faulkner's probable source for the title of his novel is the eleventh book of the *Odyssey*, in Agamemnon's speech to Odysseus about Clytemnestra's treachery. Agamemnon is relating to Odysseus how his accursed wife betrayed him with another man and then killed him at a banquet:

> . . . I, as I lay dying
> Upon the sword, raised up my hands to smite her,
> And shamelessly she turned away, and scorned
> To draw my eyelids down or close my mouth
> Though I was on the road to Hades' house.[27]

The purpose of Agamemnon's speech is to denounce the cruelty of Clytemnestra and of all women in general. In the lines which follow Agamemnon castigates Clytemnestra for plotting the murder of her lawful husband, and concludes that through this deed she has brought shame not only on herself, but on all women forever. In the context of Agamemnon's speech Faulkner's title refers to his presentation of Addie Bundren, not so much in the fact that she, like Agamemnon, "lay dying" at the beginning of the novel, but in her similarity to Clytemnestra as that character is portrayed at this point in Homer. The funeral journey is Addie's trial of her family. Her motive in exacting from Anse the promise to bury her in Jefferson is revenge, and she even seems to foresee the ordeal the Bundrens will have to undergo: "[Jewel] is my cross and he will be my salvation. He will save me from the water and from the fire." Brooks compares Addie to Lady Macbeth; both, he says, are wicked women who at once are responsible for heroic action (*The Yoknapatawpha Country,* p. 152). Indeed this particular Shakespearean play is evoked by Dewey Dell at the moment she is told of Addie's death: "I heard that my mother is dead. I wish I had time to let her die. I wish I had time to wish I had" (p. 422). It is an echo of Macbeth's reaction when he hears that Lady Macbeth is dead: "She should have died hereafter / There would have been a time for such a word." Like Dewey Dell, Macbeth feels that his wife should be mourned properly, but like Dewey Dell the forces of his own destruction are closing in and he has no time to do so.

In addition to supplying Faulkner with the title of his novel, the *Odyssey* provides other thematic parallels to *As I Lay Dying.* This same eleventh book concerns Odysseus' descent into the nether world; it is the epic hero's journey to the land of the dead, the counterpart to the Bundrens' pilgrimage to the cemetery at Jefferson. One of the souls to whom Odysseus speaks is Elpenor, whose unburied body still lay at Circe's house. His situation and Addie's are the same, and thus Elpenor begs Odysseus not to leave him "unmourned and unburied"—to which Homer's protagonist, like Anse, gives his promise that he will not. A most predominant character in the eleventh book is the seer Tiresias, whom Odysseus consults for the prediction of future events. In *As I Lay Dying* Darl, with his strange powers of clairvoyance, is a Tiresias figure. To repeat, he knows the secret of Jewel's birth and the fact of his sister's pregnancy; it is Darl who tells Jewel that Addie is going to die, who even describes the scene at the deathbed though he is not there. Dewey Dell's description of her brother specifically evokes Tiresias, both in his power of prophecy and in his blindness: Darl "that sits at the supper table with his eyes gone further than the food and the lamp, full of the land dug out of his skull and the holes filled with distance beyond the land" (p. 355). Like Faulkner's family Odysseus is tested by the old epic catastrophes, and his trial by flood may possibly be the prototype for the Bundrens' confrontation with the swollen river. In sailing from Calypso his raft is destroyed (as were Anse's wagon and mules) when Poseidon, Odysseus' enemy since he blinded his son Polyphemus, stirs up the sea in an effort to end the sailor's journey. Brought to his knees in fear, Homer's hero "speaks to his own strong spirit": "O what an unlucky man I am"; it is a cry which Anse will echo time and again in *As I Lay Dying!* Like the Bundrens, Odysseus successfully withstands his trials, and in the course of his triumph over the old epic catastrophes his motivation is no more than the Bundrens': to get back to Ithaca, to return safely again—home.

Having arrived safely in Jefferson, having buried Addie with her people and thereby fulfilled his ethical responsibility, Anse is free to pursue his own private quest. The humor involved in his successful acquisition of new teeth, a new wife, and a new gramophone does not negate the heroic gesture of the previous quest. The epic includes comedy, as W. P. Ker states; and Nestor's son reminds Menelaus of how welcome comic relief is against the grim realities portrayed in this genre: "Don't think me rude, sir, but I don't like crying over my supper." Faulkner stresses the change in Anse just before he introduces his family to the new Mrs. Bundren: The teeth "made him him look a foot taller, kind of holding his head up, hangdog and proud too" (p. 531). This completion of Anse's private quest helps to make *As I Lay Dying* (in addition to its being a novel that contains brilliantly comic passages and incidents) a comedy in the sense that the *Divine Comedy,* and the epic in general, is

a comedy—that the action moves toward success, not failure.

Neither is the heroic destroyed by the special nature of
the participants in the journey, these poor, ignorant, crass
hill farmers who see their task as a simple one—to get to
Jefferson and back home again. As Brooks says, the very
drabness of the surface of the Bundren life "is the guarantee
of the genuineness of the passion" beneath. "These people,"
he continues, "are not rhetoricians who talk themselves into
their transports" (*The Yoknapatawpha Country*, p. 165). If
the Bundrens are largely unaffected by their experience—if
they are both unaware and unconcerned that they have
performed the heroic act—we are not, and neither is
Faulkner. As he himself has said, the Bundrens are examples
of people who "pretty well coped with their fate," and fate
here is no less than "the two greatest catastrophes man can
suffer." While to them their task is a simple one, the Bundrens nevertheless have been placed in a situation which
evokes the medieval soul's pilgrimage toward salvation, the
trek of the Israelites from Egypt, and the epic hero's struggle
against the violent forces of nature. If "all they do" is to
get to Jefferson and back again, in the process they do no
less than what is required of Christian to reach the Celestial
City or the Israelites to reach the Promised Land or Odysseus to return once again safely home.

# CHAPTER IV

# Faulkner's Use of the Chivalric Romance

In interviews at Charlottesville and West Point when Faulkner was asked to list his favorite works of literature—those books which he returned to for inspiration and out of love—the answer was the same: the Old Testament, Shakespeare, the Greek tragedies—and always *Don Quixote*. Both by admission and by his definition of a writer's purpose ("to write about the human heart in conflict with itself, with Fate, and with its fellow man"), Faulkner acknowledged that "the character is the thing" and named Cervantes' knight-errant as that fictional protagonist whom he himself most loved.[1] In replying to the student who asked about the qualities that would make Don Quixote one of his favorite characters, Faulkner's answer is significant: "Admiration and pity and amusement from him—and the reason is that he is a man trying to do the best he can in this ramshackle universe he's compelled to live in. His ideals are nonsensical by our pharisaical standards, but by my standards they are not nonsensical. I can myself in Don Quixote by reading a page or two now and then, and I would like to think that my behavior is better for having read *Don Quixote*" (*Faulkner at West Point*, p. 94). The chivalric code—that ideal of love as devoted service, of honor, of loyalty to the concepts of courtesy, valor, and generosity

[115]

—especially as it is manifested in the old Don's well-intentioned but impractical attempt to redress all wrongs in the face of insurmountable odds—constitutes Faulkner's morality; it is his substitute of a social ideal in place of formal Christianity. And if there is an impasse between the world as it is and the world as it should be, if, for example, Gavin Stevens' fight with de Spain at the Christmas cotillion is in fact a quixotic defense of someone who does not want to be defended and does not need it, as Faulkner himself has said (*Faulkner in the University*, p. 141), still the allegiance of the southern writer, like that of Cervantes, is with the quester.

More than a few of Faulkner's characters function within the framework of the chivalric romance. As we have seen, Quentin, in *Absalom, Absalom!*, re-creates Judith, Bon, and Henry as protagonists of a contemporary medieval romance. Charlotte Rittenmeyer in *The Wild Palms* espouses the courtly belief in the ennobling power of love: Love endures, she says, "as long as we are worthy of keeping [it]. Good enough. Strong enough. Worthy to be allowed to keep it" (p. 88). In the narrative sequence of Ike and the cow in *The Hamlet*—an episode which has provoked much critical debate—Faulkner, in a significant experiment in fiction, has treated sodomy in terms of the conventions of the chivalric romance. In *Light in August* Byron Bunch, belying in physical appearance and in sexual prowess his most famous romantic namesake, is, as Cleanth Brooks has pointed out, a "clumsy knight-errant" on a quixotic errand (*The Yoknapatawpha Country*, p. 55). Loving Lena Grove, yet obligated, as honor dictates, to finding the father of her child, he is an unwilling Tristan to Lena's Iseult. He is presented comically, but never unsympathetically: "I took care of [Lucas Burch's] woman for him and I borned his child for him. And now there is one more thing I can do for him. I cant marry them, because I aint a minister. And I may

[116]

not can catch him, because he's got a start on me. And I may not can whip him if I do, because he is bigger than me. But I can try it. I can try to do it" (*Light in August*, p. 373).

Byron Bunch's behavior is exemplary of the most positive aspects of the courtly concept of life—an ideal of conduct which stems from Plato and reaches fruition in the troubadours. Its very value is its power to inspire to greater beauty and more honorable rules of conduct a world which seems to have lost a universal frame of reference. There is danger in such a code, however, when that code binds an individual to a fixed tradition and when it substitutes for fresh experience which demands new responses static and therefore no longer viable conventions. Robert Penn Warren perceptively recognizes and defines both these positive and negative aspects of the chivalric code: "If Faulkner feels the past as the repository of great images of human effort and integrity, he also sees it as a source of a dynamic evil. If he is aware of the romantic pull of the past, he is also aware that submission to the romance of the past is a form of death."[2]

Faulkner expressly associates this negative aspect of the chivalric code—or what I shall call, by virtue of his artistic treatment of it, the "ironic chivalric"—with that southern attitude which transforms the fact of its historic past into living legend and makes of it a glamorous if not fatal myth. Significantly it is Sir Walter Scott—that perpetrator of the nineteenth century fad for medievalism—whom another famous American writer, Mark Twain, blamed as responsible for the catastrophic fact of the Civil War. Scott had set "the world in love with dreams and phantoms," Twain asserted; "with decayed and swinish forms of religion; with decayed and degraded systems of government; with the sillinesses and emptinesses, sham grandeurs, sham gauds, and sham chivalries of a brainless and worthless long-vanished society."[3]

The mind of the southerner in the 1830s, that period

[117]

when Faulkner's Yoknapatawpha country was emerging, was particularly open to the allure of the proud and gallant gestures found in the pages of Scott's romances. In presenting the historical background of the inhabitants of his fictional county which opens *The Hamlet,* Faulkner describes a largely frontier society which is much more typical than that cultured aristocracy of the more popular magnolia myth. Migrating from England and the Scottish and Welsh marches, they were a people who made their living from the land; stratified into castes, not above vulgarity and rowdyism, they dedicated themselves to the principles of democracy and Protestantism. It was, most importantly, a nonintrospective, unintellectual society, which, as W. J. Cash points out in *The Mind of the South,* is more susceptible to an imitative style of living:

The simple man in general rarely has any considerable capacity for the real. . . . He necessarily lacks the complexity of mind, the knowledge, and, above all, the habit of skepticism essential to any generally realistic attitude. . . . He is inevitably driven back upon imagination . . . his world-construction is bound to be mainly a product of fantasy . . . his credulity is limited only by his capacity for conjuring up the unbelievable. . . . [The] primitive stuff of humanity lies very close to the surface in him . . . he likes naively to play, to expand his ego, his senses, his emotions . . . he will accept what pleases him and reject what does not . . . he displays the whole catalogue of qualities we mean by romanticism and hedonism.[4]

What is true of the simple man in general, he continues, was "perhaps even more definitely true of the Southern frontiersman by the time of the coming of the plantation." Having gradually lost the ideas and customs of that uncomplicated heritage which he had brought with him from Europe, the southerner sought a new pattern of conduct and found it in the cavalier code glorified in Scott's romances and manifested in that system of gracious living of the eighteenth-century Englishman. In examining the adaptation of this chivalric ideal, William R. Taylor points out in *Cavalier and Yankee* that there was no lack of southern contact with neoclassical England: The "invasion of the Inns of Court by prominent Southern colonials had immense consequences for Southern culture. . . . Not only did these men set standards of political and legal knowledge, they also played a significant part in implanting in the South an image of English culture in the late eighteenth century—its oratory, its literature and its manners—which, unchallenged by fresh experience, continued to dominate Southern life into the nineteenth century."[5] Thomas Sutpen, with his West Virginia mountain heritage, illustrates this allure which the chivalric held for the southerner by the particular names which he chose for his horses, his most prized possessions. Griselda, who foaled a male colt on the day Milly gave birth to his daughter, is named for Chaucer's patient heroine of medieval romance; Rob Roy, the stallion, for Scott's swashbuckling protagonist. Most important it is an example of Faulkner's use of the ironic chivalric, for Sutpen's subsequent treatment of Wash Jones's granddaughter is to be viewed as the very antithesis of the ideal of gallantry which is invoked here.

There is not, however, such a discrepancy between Sutpen's actual behavior and his pretensions toward the chivalric code as may appear, and this is precisely the danger Mark Twain saw in the Walter Scott romances. The prewar South was still largely a frontier society; the first and second generation aristocrats could put on, like a garment as Cash says (and the metaphor is significant), the pattern of gracious manner and gallant gesture; but the fact remained that they were only a pseudo aristocracy, without the tradition of the culture they imitated—without "the aristocrat's experience

. . . the calm certainty, bred of that experience, which is the aristocratic manner's essential warrant" (*The Mind of the South*, p. 71). As Cash points out, a frequent result of the impact of an aristocratic manner on frontier individualism is an ideal which expresses itself in violence—of wounded honor which settles its own account by duels or by lynching. Faulkner's fullest treatment of violence as component of the chivalric code of conduct is to be found in his presentation of the John Sartoris myth, which will be discussed at length later. Let it suffice now to say that Drusilla, who by all rights should assume the role of the lady in the chivalric romance, becomes, by virtue of Faulkner's ironic treatment, an instrument of revenge in defiance of her sex. It is Drusilla—with her close-cropped hair and with her fame as warrior in the colonel's cavalry—who hands Bayard the two duelling pistols, "the Greek amphora priestess of a succinct and formal violence" (*The Unvanquished*, p. 252).

With the Civil War the southerner found his dream of the ideal society defeated, his code of manners useless. Faced with Reconstruction he looked not to the future, but to the past for stability and security—as "a shield," Bayard says in *The Unvanquished*, "between ourselves and reality, between us and fact and doom" (p. 4). Faced with the experience of evil and the experience of tragedy—which, as C. Vann Woodward states, "are parts of the Southern heritage that are as difficult to reconcile with the American legend of innocence and social felicity as the experience of poverty and defeat are to reconcile with the legends of abundance and success"[6]—the southerner after the Civil War submerged the fact of guilt and defeat and at the same time romanticized the old aristocratic claim of the planter. In this process of translating southern fact into southern legend, the Confederate cause and the defeat itself became glamorous, and in *Sartoris* they are significantly identified with the doomed yet gallant chivalric battle of Charlemagne and Roland at Roncevaux. That same cavalier code which the prewar southerner had used as a pattern of conduct became for the postwar southerner a retreat into a golden age of superb if not reckless heroism. By naming all six of his middle-aged but unmarried sons after the generals of Lee's army, Pappy MacCallum—Faulkner's backwoods patriarch who embodies the practical yeoman code of simple dignity and propriety—is evidence of this perpetuation of the past on the present. But because they are able successfully to cope with their fate, the MacCallums are examples, in Warren's terms, of those who see the past as repository of images of human effort and integrity, yet who are still able to function effectively in the present. The danger, however, is in the individual who loses his identity in the romantic pull of the past. Mrs. Vickery expresses the dilemma very well: "Instead of days filled with new experiences arousing new reactions, they relive the lives of their ancestors; instead of gathering memories for their own old age, they devote themselves to remembering and so preserving legends of a past they have never seen" (*Novels,* p. 262).

To the Reverend Gail Hightower, the disgraced ex-minister in *Light in August,* the figure of his grandfather who was killed in Van Dorn's cavalry raid on Grant's stores in Jefferson embodies that cavalier heroism which is painfully lacking in his own life. The reality of the fact that his grandfather was killed while stealing chickens from a Confederate roost Hightower significantly chooses to ignore: "I believe. I know. . . . It's too fine, too simple, ever to have been invented." The Negro Cinthy describes the incident as it really is, as Faulkner means for us to see it, that of a schoolboy's foolish prank, and we can imagine his tone—full of commonsense, and so incredulous and a bit disgusted too:

"Stealin' chickens. A man growed . . . gone to a war whar his business was killin' Yankees, killed in somebody else's henhouse wid a han'ful of feathers." Hightower, however, is committed to his imaginative construction of his grandfather as the stuff from which legends are made, and thus he translates even this schoolboy's prank into an act of heroic bravura: "It may have been a woman, likely enough the wife of a Confederate soldier. I like to think so. It's fine so. Any soldier can be killed by the enemy in the heat of battle. . . . But not with a shotgun, a fowling piece, in a henhouse" (pp. 424–25).

Having created such a glamorous legend, Hightower falls victim to it. He has no identity apart from that cavalier figure which represents for him all the gallantry and courage and honor of a romantic past. "I have not even been clay," Hightower thinks to himself; "I have been a single instant of darkness in which a horse galloped and a gun crashed" (p. 430). The old minister admits that his reason for coming to Jefferson was not through duty to his congregation but because of his fierce desire to "return to the place . . . where my life had already ceased before it began. . . . My life died there, was shot from the saddle of a galloping horse in a Jefferson street one night twenty years before it was ever born." And when that same congregation dismisses him because of the scandal of his wife's suicide, Hightower buries himself inside his lonely house, his "sanctuary" as he calls it, where he could be "sheltered from the harsh gale of living and die so, peacefully" (pp. 418–19), and spends his days at his window watching for the galloping hooves of his grandfather's horse.

To the extent that Hightower chooses to live in time that stopped twenty years before his birth, in the company of one memory safe from change and violation, to that extent does he deny his responsibility to the "living people" (p. 53)

—to his wife and his parishioners. The preacher admits to himself that he substituted for "the crucified shape of pity and love, a swaggering and unchastened bravo killed with a shotgun in a peaceful henhouse" (p. 428). By delivering from his pulpit sermons of "God and salvation and the galloping horses and his dead grandfather" (p. 56), Hightower confesses that it was not to his congregation that he preached each Sunday, to those "faces full of bafflement and hunger and eagerness . . . waiting to believe" (p. 427), and in doing so he acknowledges that he as preacher has failed. Similarly, by admitting that all he ever wanted to be was his own dead grandfather on the instant of his death, Hightower confesses that he refused to help his wife when she needed it and in his neglect perhaps became "her seducer and her murderer, author and instrument of her shame and death" (p. 430). Hightower is redeemed at that moment when he asserts his identity outside the legend and dares to participate in the life around him. The old minister is willing to lie in a vain attempt to save Joe Christmas's life, knowing that the lie is tantamount to an admission of homosexuality. Most important, he helps deliver Lena Grove's baby. After its delivery the old man, for the first time in many years, knows what it is like to have a purpose. "I ought to feel worse than I do," he thinks, and then, after going over again in his mind what he has accomplished, "I showed them. . . . Life comes to the old man yet, while they get there too late. . . . What if I do? What if I do feel it? triumph and pride? What if I do?" (pp. 354–55). The preacher leaves his sanctuary and walks outside to the woods. "Smelling the savage and fecund odor of the earth," Hightower thinks about Lena and her destiny: *The good stock peopling in tranquil obedience to it the good earth; from these hearty loins without hurry or haste descending mother and daughter"* (p. 356). It is an affirmation of the life force, which also becomes an affirmation of living. Because Hightower has dared to become involved in life and because he has dared to see himself not as his grandfather's ghost, but as he really is and accept the responsibility for his failings, the old minister is finally rewarded with the vision long sought-after: "They rush past . . . with brandished arms, beneath whipping ribbons from slanted and eager lances. . . . He still hears . . . the wild bugles and the clashing sabres and the dying thunder of hooves" (pp. 431–32). Because Hightower has atoned for his sins, the vision comes no longer as romantic escape (as some critics have maintained)[7] but as exultation.

Faulkner's fullest treatment of the ironic chivalric is in his presentation of the Sartoris code of conduct. Like Hightower the Sartorises see the southern past as a repository of romantic heroism; they then go a step further and see in the past an ideal of conduct and demand of one another a pattern of behavior which will conform to the conventions of this ideal. That code of behavior which Colonel John Sartoris, the progenitor of the line, passes on to his male descendants, which Bayard knows to be "not something which [the colonel] possessed but something which he had bequeathed us which we could never forget" (*The Unvanquished*, p. 291), is based not on that chivalric concept of life which is positive and which constitutes Faulkner's morality but on self-destructive pride and violence and cavalier recklessness; it is most foolishly and most romantically embodied in the action of the Carolina Bayard, who was killed while trying to capture the enemy's anchovies to give to General Lee.

Even Aunt Jenny, the lone voice of practicality in the Sartoris line who stubbornly maintains that "heroics are for boys or fool young women," falls prey to the glamorous allure of the code. It is she who tells the story of the Carolina

Bayard and Jeb Stuart, that plumed figure of courteous gallantry. Over the years the tale grows richer, as she transforms the prank of two young men into a legend of courage and honor and derring-do until it becomes in its universal moral significance almost a myth of salvation: "As she grew older the tale itself grew richer and richer, taking on a mellow splendor like wine; until what had been a hair-brained prank of two heedless and reckless boys wild with their own youth had become a gallant and finely tragical focal point to which the history of the race had been raised from out the old miasmic swamps of spiritual sloth by two angels valiantly fallen and strayed, altering the course of human events and purging the souls of men" (*Sartoris*, p. 9). By the extreme foolhardiness of a quest after anchovies, by the humiliating fact that the Carolina Bayard was shot in the back by a cook, Faulkner undercuts Aunt Jenny's telling of the tale just as he undercut Hightower's heroic presentation of his grandfather; he is emphasizing the discrepancy between how life really is and how the Sartorises choose to interpret it and to live it. General Stuart's final evaluation of the Carolina Bayard is also Faulkner's pronouncement on the chivalric code of behavior as it is practiced by the Sartoris family: "He [Stuart] always spoke well of Bayard. He said he was a good officer and a fine cavalryman, but that he was too reckless" (*Sartoris*, p. 18).

Besides this outrageous bravado inherent in the Sartoris code there is a second and more important component in the family's pattern of behavior. It is an ideal which expresses itself in violence, which is the Sartorises' own exaggeration of what Cash calls the impact of an aristocratic manner on frontier individualism. When old man Falls, in *Sartoris*, describes the colonel's shooting of the two carpetbaggers who wanted to vote, he describes it reverently, as the heroic act which eliminated a dangerous threat to the

glorious Confederate cause. Falls's adoration of John
Sartoris, almost to the point of deifying him, is expressed
in the old man's wish to be metamorphosed into the colonel's victims: "I sort of envied them two Nawthuners, be
damned ef I didn't. A feller kin take a wife and live with
her fer a long time, but after all they ain't no kin. But the
feller that brings you into the world or sends you outen hit"
(p. 236). When this same act is mentioned by Joanna Burden (the victims are her grandfather and her brother) in
*Light in August,* it is described as Faulkner means for us
to see it—as the senseless murder of "an old onearmed man
and a boy who had never even cast his first vote" (p. 218).
For the Sartorises the result of following a code of violence
is that it frequently ends in their own death; they become
victims of the myth they have created. If Rosa Millard's
quest to recover her silver, her horses, and her slaves is not
quite as foolish as that of the Carolina Bayard, it is nevertheless just as fatal. In *Sartoris* the fourth generation Bayard
is to be seen as the traditional romantic hero as he is conceived by Byron. Having failed in World War 1 to emulate
those acts of glamorous self-destruction which distinguished
his ancestors in the Civil War, young Bayard exhibits the
Byronic hero's brooding melancholy and wishes for his own
death. Lying in bed one night, Bayard thinks, "Three score
and ten, the Bible said. Seventy years. And he was only
twenty-six. Not much more than a third through it. Hell"
(p. 160). It is fitting, then, that an allusion to Roncevaux
should end *Sartoris.* It is an evocation of gallant yet foolish
self-sacrifice, and as such it anticipates the end of the family
line which shapes its behavior after this particular chivalric
pattern.

Faulkner's attitude toward the Sartoris code of conduct
is expressed in "An Odor of Verbena," which was written
especially for *The Unvanquished.* With the death of Colo-

[126]

nel John Sartoris, Bayard, his son, becomes "The Sartoris" (p. 247). The title obligates Bayard to act in accordance with the family's code and demands of him that he redress his father's murder by slaying Redmond. It is the same pattern of violence and reckless bravado to which Bayard had earlier and unquestioningly conformed, when, as a young boy, he had nailed Grumby's right hand to Granny Millard's grave. It is at that moment, however, when he realizes the Sartoris code is contrary to everything the Bible preaches (the one book, Ike McCaslin says in "The Bear," whose transcribers attempt to write down "the universal truths of the heart") that Bayard speaks for Faulkner. "If there was anything at all in the Book," Bayard thinks, "anything of hope and peace for His blind and bewildered spawn which He had chosen above all others to offer immortality, *Thou shalt not kill* must be it" (p. 249). By confronting Redmond unarmed, Bayard repudiates the Sartoris code of retribution. It is the most heroic action of the book, exemplary of those concepts of courage, bravery, and honor which Faulkner associates with chivalry as positive ideal. Most important Bayard acts according to his own moral conscience: "I must live with myself, you see" (p. 276). And this is the danger in the Sartoris code—or any code that demands a pattern of behavior in conformity to conventions of the past—that it makes moral choice impossible. This is what Aunt Jenny discovers in *Sartoris* in the recognition scene at the family graveyard. Looking at the stone effigy of the old colonel—that image of "swashbuckling vainglory"—she realizes it dominates the other graves, just as the memory of the man in death dominates his living descendants—"that arrogant shade which [held sway over] the house and the life that went on there" (p. 113). By virtue of being the original Sartoris, the progenitor of the family code, the colonel achieves a kind of immortality, since he establishes the pattern of behavior to be

[127]

imitated by each succeeding generation. By the same token he dooms his descendants by depriving them of ever asserting their own personalities outside this prescribed code of conduct. Thus the repetition of the names John and Bayard, bestowed on each generation, has the effect of obliterating individuality; it binds each to upholding not only a family name but a tradition of behavior as well. Like Hightower in *Light in August* it remains for Bayard in *The Unvanquished* to assert his identity outside the pull of the romantic past, and like Hightower he does not go unrewarded. On Bayard's pillow Drusilla places the single sprig of verbena as accolade to his bravery—"the only scent you could smell above the smell of horses and courage" (p. 253).

If Gail Hightower commits an injustice against the code of chivalry to the extent that he uses it as comfortable escape into a romantic cavalier past, if the Sartorises pervert the code by substituting for its principles their own pattern of reckless bravura and glamorous self-destruction, Quentin Compson seeks to preserve the chivalric code as it was nobly conceived by Plato and practiced by Cervantes' don as an ideal of behavior in the twentieth century. Quentin sees the chivalric ideal as the codification of those virtuous qualities of bravery, of loyalty to the concepts of courtesy and generosity, especially as those qualities are directed toward devoted service to women and defense of their honor.[8] Cleanth Brooks calls Quentin "a classical instance of the courtly lover" (*The Yoknapatawpha Country*, p. 332); and from the time he was a small boy, when he fought his schoolmate for putting a frog in his teacher's desk, the young protagonist of *The Sound and the Fury* exhibits the medieval knight's devotion to the protection of his women. By espousing the chivalric code as a pattern of behavior, Quentin hopes to inspire his family to more honorable rules of conduct, and if he fails he will at least have invested the disintegration of the Compson family—an alcoholic father, a neurotic mother, a promiscuous sister, an idiot brother—with the heroic dimensions associated with this ideal. Quentin's espousal of the code is his answer to the nihilistic philosophy of his father. Believing that there is no meaning in anything, Mr. Compson undercuts the chivalric pattern of conduct by seeing it as the foolish defense of a principle that does not even exist: "Because [virginity] means less to women, Father said. . . . It's like death: only a state in which the others are left and I said, But to believe it doesn't matter and he said, That's what's so sad about anything: not only virginity" (*The Sound and the Fury*, p. 97).

Quentin's flaw is that ultimately the abstract chivalric code becomes more important to him than the reality of daily living; the chivalric pattern comes to mean more than the living individuals whose conduct that ideal should inspire. In the appendix to *The Sound and the Fury* Faulkner says that Quentin "loved not his sister's body" but the concept of virginity which that body represented (p. 9). Brooks's designation of Quentin as "the most extreme devotee of the Tristan myth" (*The Yoknapatawpha Country*, p. 205) is indeed appropriate. Like Tristan, Quentin does not love Caddy but loves instead the abstract ideal of love, the condition of being in love; and like Tristan, Quentin welcomes the sword that is the barrier to consummation, for it prevents the actual expression of love on its living object. Thus Quentin's desire for incest remains simply a desire; it is never fulfilled. Moreover the very nature of this love—that of brother for sister—bars its expression in Western culture. Quentin's willingness to join the scores of chivalric lovers before him who have been sentenced to Purgatory—the consequence of this sin of incest—is really a wish to be isolated with Caddy in the "clean flame of Hell

[129]

. . . out of the loud world" (p. 195). It is a desire for death, which is the ultimate obstacle, Denis de Rougemont says, to the fulfillment of love.[9] And again in the appendix Faulkner says that what Quentin loved above all was death; he anticipates it, Faulkner continues, as the lover joyously anticipates the body of his beloved—and the comparison is significant: "Who loved death above all, who loved only death, loved and lived in a deliberate and almost perverted anticipation of death as a lover loves and deliberately refrains from the waiting willing friendly tender incredible body of his beloved, until he can no longer bear not the refraining but the restraint and so flings, hurls himself, relinquishing, drowning" (pp. 9–10).

There are, of course, in Quentin's section several references to Hamlet. If Faulkner means for us to see in Quentin anything of Shakespeare's character, it is in Quentin's similarity to that figure which emerges from the popular misconception of Shakespeare's hero—a brooding, sensitive young man so paralyzed by battles with his conscience that he is unable to act. Quentin can function quite well on a verbal level. Indeed when we read Quentin's section, we are struck at how much of that section is given over to the fictional narrator's conversations with his father, to his tortured reveries of the past. This itself is the very nature of Quentin's difficulty—an inability to operate beyond this verbal level, to translate, as it were, the formalized principles of his code of conduct into significant action. Quentin's reaction to the outrage he feels at Caddy's engagement to Herbert Head, for example, is only an imagined duel in which he appropriately fancies himself shooting not the boorish fiancé but instead the fiancé's voice (p. 124). Similarly in his desire to accomplish the ultimate sin—"something so dreadful that they would have fled hell except us" (p. 98)—Quentin is finally forced to admit to his father that he only said he committed incest, that in actuality he "was afraid to [approach Caddy] . . . was afraid she might" (p. 195).

Quentin's abortive fight with Dalton Ames over Caddy's honor is the one heroic act in which he dares to give expression to the chivalric principles which he espouses. Michael Millgate in *The Achievement of William Faulkner* perceptively points out that whenever Quentin does act, his concern is for "the act's significance as a gesture rather than for its practical efficacy" (p. 96). The subsequent fight with Gerald Bland, then, is important to Quentin only in its symbolic aspect—as duplication of the earlier fight with Ames, which, in turn, is important as an act of honor defended. In view of the fact that Quentin is so soundly defeated by Ames (embarrassed, he realizes he has not even been hit by Ames, but has "just passed out like a girl"), the stereotyped romantic edict which he gives his antagonist is more than a little comic, but it is an ultimatum which his role demands—"I'll give you until sundown to leave town" (p. 178).

As his confrontation with Ames demonstrates, Quentin is, in the final analysis, ineffectual; he fails to live up to the courtly role which he has assigned himself. We must look at the Quentin Compson in *Absalom, Absalom!* and his relationship in that novel to Henry Sutpen in order to comprehend fully Quentin's own awareness of his inadequacy. When he and Shreve try to reconstruct the pieces of the Sutpen story, it is Henry who fires Quentin's imagination, so much so that the young storyteller becomes one with the shade he is re-creating. The identification is so complete that the fictional narrator imagines a composite figure, Henry-Quentin, riding out to Sutpen's Hundred on that December night in 1859 to introduce Bon to Judith. Because Quentin wants to identify himself with Henry but can participate in this identification only up to a point, it makes the fact of his own failure that much more difficult to bear; for Henry, unlike Quentin, is able to fire the shot that ends the threat to his sister's honor, and by doing so he succeeds, where Quentin does not, in performing the heroic act.

If Quentin is unable to fulfill the obligations of his chivalric code, still he is unwilling to renounce that code. When he recognizes the impasse between life as it is lived by the Compsons and his own principles of honor and gallantry, he takes his life. It is as Mr. Compson had predicted—that Quentin will not commit suicide until he comes "to believe that even she [Caddy] was not quite worth despair" (p. 196). Although by all practical standards Quentin fails to live up to the heroic role, nevertheless Faulkner's fullest sympathy is with the quester; Quentin's chivalric attitude is to be positively evaluated against Dalton Ames's pronouncement on women which immediately follows his confrontation with Quentin: "Theyre all bitches" (p. 179). Faulkner's attitude toward his young protagonist is further clarified by his presentation of another Compson who patterns her conduct after the code of chivalry. The role to which Caroline Compson adapts her behavior—with more than a little joy, one must think—is the stereotyped role of the southern lady who is placed on a pedestal. The fact that she is one of those "delicately nurtured Southern ladies" (p. 241) allows Mrs. Compson the excuse to indulge herself in her numerous attacks of hypochondria. As with Quentin the role commands certain behavior, and so Benjy, who was named at birth after her own family, must be rechristened upon her discovery that he is an idiot so as not to bring shame to the Bascomb line. Similarly, when Mrs. Compson sees the youth kissing her fifteen-year-old Caddy, she reacts as she believes her image demands: "And all the next day she went around the house in a black dress and a veil . . . crying and saying her little daughter was dead" (p. 247). If Mrs. Compson presents a humorous picture garbed in her mourning dress, confident that God will not flout her because she is, after all, a lady, she has none of the author's sympathy that is sometimes associated with a comic presentation. The significant difference between Quentin and his mother in terms of their chivalric pattern of behavior is that Quentin retains the conception of the morally valid principles which underlies this code of conduct while Mrs. Compson does not. She very willingly accepts the devoted service and protection due a southern lady, since nothing could be more pleasing to her lazy, self-centered nature; at the same time she relegates to Dilsey the matriarch's role of family stabilizer and moral center. The result of Mrs. Compson's withholding from her family the love and affection, the attention and the discipline they need is revealed in Quentin's poignant cry before he drowns himself in the Charles River: *"If I'd just had a mother so I could say Mother Mother"* (p. 190).

When asked about the peculiar structure of his double novel *The Wild Palms*, Faulkner replied that it was originally "one story—the story of Charlotte Rittenmeyer and Harry Wilbourne, who sacrificed everything for love, and then lost that." After he had started the book, he said that he "realized suddenly that something was missing, it needed emphasis, something to lift it like counterpoint in music. So I wrote on the "Old Man" story until "The Wild Palms" story rose back to pitch. . . . Then I raised it to pitch again with another section of its antithesis, which is the story of a man who got his love and spent the rest of the book fleeing from it."[10] The basic link between the two stories is the theme of love as it is portrayed in the pages of medieval literature. "Wild Palms" is the story of two people who struggle to preserve the romantic ideal at a time when there is no longer any belief in a world well lost for love. Since the tone is deliberately antiromantic, it is perhaps less easy to see in "Old Man" the chivalric mode. Nevertheless the task which the tall convict is called upon to perform is the knight's archetypal quest in the medieval romance—the overcoming of physical obstacles in order to rescue the lady in distress.

The action of "Wild Palms" takes place outside of Yoknapatawpha County, apart from Faulkner's rural countryside of Frenchman's Bend. The setting is particularly modern, and there is the implication that the contemporary scene has somehow degenerated from a more glorious time. "We have eliminated [love]," Harry Wilbourne says to his friend McCord, in an elegy to the twentieth century. "If Venus returned she would be a soiled man in a subway lavatory with a palm full of French post-cards" (p. 136). What Harry and Charlotte wish to do is to experience once again that grand passion which existed before it was tamed and tarnished by modern day standards of conventionality, standards, Harry realizes with horror, that have "forced [men and women] to conform to the pattern of human life which has now evolved to do without love" (p. 140). One product of this pattern of behavior is the sterile figure of the Baptist doctor who rents Charlotte and Harry the cabin on the gulf shore. Having "married the wife his father had picked out for him" and having slept with her for twenty-three childless years, he not only has accepted society's standards, he becomes their mouthpiece: he is outraged that Harry and Charlotte are not married, incredulous that Harry himself has performed the abortion. He is clearly Harry's foil; his destiny could so easily have been Harry's too had Wilbourne not met Charlotte.

Like Charles Bon and other chivalric lovers before him, Harry's finding the object of his love seems ordained by either Fate or Circumstance. Harry's roommate Flint accidentally opens Wilbourne's birthday telegram, and the second-hand invitation to the party where Harry meets Charlotte follows. Faulkner himself associates the meeting with the forces of "destiny"—or "ill-luck, since otherwise [Harry] might have discovered that love no more exists just at one spot and in one moment and in one body out of all the earth and all time and all the teeming breathed, than sunlight does" (p. 43). But, as Cleanth Brooks points out, romantic love always means the discovery of the *one* person out of all others, this certain person and no other.[11] Having brought about their meeting, Fate intervenes a second time; it is at that moment when Harry and Charlotte must accept the termination of their relationship because they have no money. At this point Harry finds the wallet in the trash bin. It is Saturday afternoon; the post office is closed, and he is therefore unable to return it to the owner.

It is Charlotte who initiates Harry into a life lived in accord with a romantic ideal, expressed in her wish for it "to be all honeymoon, always" (p. 83). Although she frequently talks of her enjoyment of what she calls bitching, her concept of love is as ennobling as that celebrated in medieval love lyrics. Love "doesn't die," she tells Harry. "It just leaves you, goes away, if you are not good enough, worthy enough" (p. 83). How much their relationship is elevated above the fleshly is evidenced by the fact that they do not consummate their love in the dingy hotel room, an incident notable for its comic portrayal of the stereotyped tryst as it is conceived in our time—the carrying around in a suitcase of bricks carefully wrapped in a towel, the signing of the two fictitious names in the hotel register. Neither do they have sexual relations in the cabin in Utah, though the Buckners enjoy their cravings in "stallion-like" coupling.

At the beginning of the story Harry is remarkably un-

[135]

touched by experience. He pursues his medical degree with
the same fanatical determination and ascetic dedication as
that demonstrated by Labove, and significantly Faulkner
uses the image of the monk to describe them both. A virgin
at twenty-seven, Harry acknowledges that he has willingly
repudiated love. While Charlotte desires to drown herself
in one passionately felt experience, Harry appropriately envi-
sions himself as a figure lying "passively on his back as
though he floated effortless and without volition upon an
unreturning stream" (p. 34). Like the Baptist doctor Wilbourne is a product of his puritan heritage, and on the way
to the drawing room where he and Charlotte are to consummate their love he is overcome by feelings of guilt; he imagines everyone in the train watching them pass, intuiting
their destination, since he is convinced the two "must have
disseminated an aura of unsanctity and disaster like a smell"
(p. 60). Under Charlotte's tutelage, however, Harry gradually commits himself to a romantic ideal. "She has marked
me too forever," he tells McCord (p. 133). His is the long
diatribe against bourgeois respectability; his too the decision
to leave Chicago, since in becoming a part of a routine of
work, of being paid for work which leaves them no time for
one another, they are becoming a part of that very system
"which has now evolved to do without love." The sin is
compounded by the very nature of Harry's vocation, since
in writing true confession stories for pulp magazines, Wilbourne is making a travesty of the very ideal he espouses.

Charlotte and Harry's relationship is marked by that isolation which characterizes the union of all great lovers
throughout history. It is a condition which both fervently
desire. Like Quentin who wishes to be isolated with Caddy
in the "clean flame of Hell, out of the loud world," Harry
and Charlotte are also beguiled by *the passionate idea of
[their being] two damned and doomed and isolated forever*

[136]

*against the world and God"* (p. 82). During their Edenic idyll on the Wisconsin lake Charlotte calls Harry "Adam." It is her own deliberate identification of the two of them with the original lovers in Eden. Such an identification evokes not only the idea of unfallen passion but the complete and total solitude of the first parents. This isolation, while it is desired, is also the consequence of the special nature of their love. "I am afraid," Harry tells McCord before he and Charlotte leave for Utah (p. 139). It is a fear which comes at the moment he realizes the danger in refusing to conform to a world which has eliminated love: *"You are born submerged in anonymous lockstep with the teeming anonymous myriads of your time and generation; you get out of step once, falter once, and you are trampled to death"* (p. 54). Harry and Charlotte's odyssey from New Orleans to Chicago to Utah and back again to New Orleans becomes a desperate attempt at flight. Appropriately the journey ends where it began. To renounce the harsh world of reality is not such an easy task; to survive Charlotte and Harry must somehow manage to cope with it: "You live *in* sin," Charlotte says to Wilbourne; "you cant live on it" (p. 83).

In "Wild Palms" Charlotte and Harry are as doomed as any star-crossed lovers of chivalric romances which end tragically. *"There are rules!"* the Baptist doctor thinks to himself when he discovers it was the lover who performed the abortion. *"Limits! To fornication, adultery, to abortion, crime* and what he meant was *To that of love and passion and tragedy which is allowed to anyone lest he become as God Who has suffered likewise all that Satan can have known"* (p. 280). In the doctor's cry of outrage is the implication that Harry and Charlotte have overstepped not only the laws of their society but those of God and Nature as well, and because they have done so they, like Sutpen, are destroyed. Because Charlotte and Harry have "sacrificed everything for love and then lost that," many see "Wild Palms" as Faulkner's warning against the folly in such a romantic approach to life. Charlotte's death literally is the result of an act of love. Wilbourne realizes he bungles the abortion because he loves Charlotte; he is like the *"miser* [who] *would probably bungle the blowing of his own safe"* (p. 297). Walter Slatoff focuses on the dilemma when he says that he fails to see any meaning in Charlotte's death; Wilbourne, he maintains, seems to have learned nothing from his harrowing experience.[12] The Harry Wilbourne at the end of the story, however, is a vastly different man from what we know him to be at the beginning. He finally discovers what Charlotte has known all along—"that love and suffering are the same thing and that the value of love is the sum of what you have to pay for it" (p. 48). For much of his life Wilbourne has been unwilling to pay the price. Before he meets Charlotte he chooses to repudiate love because he feels by doing so it will give him peace, leave him free to float "effortless and without volition upon an unreturning stream." And even after he has been marked by Charlotte, Harry is still not strong enough to risk the suffering. When he finds out she wants him to perform the abortion he insists that there must be an easier way out: *"It cant be this difficult,"* he thinks, *"this much of a price"* (p. 208). But when he throws away the cyanide tablet, he at last realizes he can bear to live: *"Not could. Will. I want to"* (p. 324). Like Charlotte he is ready to associate love with suffering. Having had the privilege of the one, he has the courage to endure the agony of the other: *"Yes,"* he says, *"between grief and nothing I will take grief"* (p. 324).

Clearly in its comic mode "Old Man" is the antithesis of "Wild Palms"; it is the story, as Faulkner has said, of someone who *does* succeed in getting his love, and who then spends the rest of the book running away from it. There is no longer any need, as there was in 1939 when *The Wild Palms* appeared, to explain the peculiar structure of the double novel. Critics in very perceptive and detailed analyses have justified the coupling of the stories.[13] By and large, however, these commentators have shown "Wild Palms" and "Old Man" to be complementary by focusing on the diametric opposition of the two stories. For example Olga Vickery sees in the figure of the tall convict Harry Wilbourne's foil. The instinctive, intuitive protagonist of "Old Man" to her suggests "an almost pre-conscious state of existence." While the convict has no time to fear what might happen to him since all his energy is directed toward trying to cope with "purely physical phenomena which demand certain physical responses," Harry Wilbourne nearly goes insane as he thinks of the diminishing row of cans left in the cupboard. Wilbourne, constantly anticipating his own defeat, is a victim of his own introspection (*Novels*, pp. 159, 161–62). Mrs. Vickery's observation is indeed true up to a point. Certainly we are meant to measure Charlotte's romantic desire to drown in the ocean against the tall convict's literal desperate attempt not to. But we must not forget that at one point in his life the convict was just as seduced by romantic notions as Charlotte and Wilbourne. His ill-fated decision to rob the train had come from reading detective novels, whose writers lead people to believe in the success of "the Diamond Dicks and Jesse Jameses" (p. 23). His motive for the robbery is equally romantic—he does it to impress his sweetheart: in doing so, "who to know what Capone's uncandled bridehood she might not have dreamed to be her destiny and fate" (p. 338). The tall convict's romantic attitude points to a most important similarity between the two stories, which further allows us to appreciate the particular alternating structure of *The Wild Palms*. What the two have in com-

[139]

mon is the chivalric mode. In "Old Man" Faulkner has ingeniously cast in the role of modern-day knight someone who has no desire at all to be a courtly hero.

The medieval knight's rescue of the lady in distress has its counterpart in the tall convict's mission to return to safety the woman on the cypress snag. The convict himself entertains the romantic possibilities in such a task, until that moment when the fact of the woman's pregnancy eradicates whatever maidens he had "dreamed of rescuing from what craggy pinnacle or dragoned keep" (p. 149). The fact of the pregnancy is of course humorous in intent, but it also serves to show that the convict's motive is purely selfless; the claiming of the lady, which traditionally ends the knight's quest, will be denied to him. While the knight's rewards are thus forbidden, the obstacles which hinder the successful completion of the quest are not. The tall convict's confrontation with the flood is every bit as violent as the Bundrens' ordeal, and it is described in terms of the same apocalyptic imagery: thus the convict feels himself "being toyed with by a current of water going nowhere, beneath a day which would wane toward no evening"; overhead the lightning flashes while the water rolls on, "ridged with dirty *phosphorescent* foam and filled with a debris of destruction" (pp. 147, 159; italics mine). The outrage which the convict is made to endure is further compounded by the fact that he must cope with the flood not just once, but three times, the third time coming just when he has attained some degree of peace and contentment; hunting alligators with the Cajun, he has only a brief interlude to remember what a privilege it is to be allowed to work and earn money before the dynamite blows up the levee and the deluge returns. The tall convict is as victimized by the human community as he is by the forces of nature. In his attempt to fulfill his obligation and deliver up his charge he is twice fired upon for his effort—once by a band of criminals in a shanty boat and again by a group of soldiers near Baton Rouge. In his own way the tall convict suffers just as much as Harry Wilbourne, though he is unable to articulate his anguish. His reaction to the soldiers' gunfire is an inarticulate cry, which Faulkner appropriately compares to the scream of a dying rabbit:—"an indictment of all breath and its folly and suffering, its infinite capacity for folly and pain" (p. 174).

Alone on the wide expanse of water the tall convict and the pregnant woman are as isolated from the loud world as Harry and Charlotte. There is an important difference here, however, for the isolation of the lovers in "Wild Palms" is a condition of their special relationship and, as such, it is intently desired. Their flight from society is self-imposed, and it is to be measured against the tall convict's desperate attempt to be reinstated in the human community: "I want to surrender!" the tall convict screams as he dodges the soldiers' bullets. "All in the world I want is just to surrender" (pp. 173–74). Although he fervently wants to return to the safe orderly world he had known at Parchman, he will not do so until he fulfills his obligation. Thus he realizes with a kind of impotent fury that the reason the plump convict was hurled safely into a tree while he was forced to remain on the treacherous water was because the arbiter of human affairs "knew that he alone of the two of them would make any attempt to return and rescue his companion" (p. 146). This concept of honor, integral to all tales of chivalry, operates throughout "Old Man." The tall convict refuses to board the steamboat or leave the Cajun hut if, in so doing, he has to abandon the skiff, which, like the woman, is also in his trust. The act arouses no praise from the deputy at Parchman, but instead only an incredulous amazement. "He even brought that damn boat back," the deputy says in disbelief. "If he'd a throwed the boat away he could a walked back in three days" (p. 326). But the deputy himself continually acts out of expediency, and honor-bound gestures are lost on him. Similarly the convict will not take the money from the doctor on the steamboat, just as he refuses the oar the Cajun offers him, although he desperately needs a replacement for the lost paddle. More important, in terms of the story's chivalric framework, the tall convict displays a respect for his charge which is not at all unlike the knight's reverence of his lady. Much to the disapproving amazement of the plump convict, the protagonist of "Old Man" refrains from having sexual relations with his female companion, though it has been two years since he has had a woman: "There were times, seconds, at first when if it had not been for the baby he might have, might have tried. But they were just seconds because in the next instant his whole being would seem to flee the very idea in a kind of savage and horrified revulsion" (pp. 334–35).

In light of the tall convict's chivalrous behavior, he is not such a foil to Harry Wilbourne as may first appear. Their biographies in certain respects are strikingly similar. Like Harry the tall convict at the beginning of the story is largely untouched by experience. He too is the ascetic; his seven years in the penitentiary at Parchman is, for him, a "monastic existence of shotguns and shackles" (p. 153) where he is secure from all pregnant and female life. Wilbourne's image of himself as a figure lying effortlessly on his back upon an unreturning stream also describes the convict, who "still and would ever be no more than the water bug upon the surface of the pond" (p. 266). As in Harry and Charlotte's relationship, it is the woman who initiates the tall convict into the experience of living. All along she has been wiser than he. When she is giving birth on the snake-infested island, the convict runs to get the tin can at her instruction, scoops it full of water, then holds it up for her to drink—until she tells him better. What the woman teaches the tall convict is essentially what Charlotte taught Harry—"that love and suffering are the same thing and that the value of love is the sum of what you have to pay for it." The convict discovers that the cause of all his anguish is not the flood—since when it was done with him "it would spew him back into the comparatively safe world he had been snatched violently out of" (p. 147)—but the woman. After the birth on the island—at which time not only the baby but, in a sense, the convict too is born into the world of experience—he looks down at the woman and her child and realizes that *this is what severed me violently from all I ever knew and did not wish to leave and cast me upon a medium I was born to fear"* (p. 231). The tall convict's relationship not just with the woman in the tree, but with each of the other women with whom he has contact in the story, is marked by some degree of suffering on his part. While a sense of honor prevents him from committing any violation against his charge, the convict does have sexual relations with the wife of one of the men who works with him in the sawmill, and the act costs him his job. The story ends with the convict's antiromantic expletive about women in general, which is precipitated by the memory of his sweetheart, for whom he is willing to go to prison and from whom, in recompense for all his trouble, he receives the hastily scrawled postcard sent to him from her honeymoon.

Having learned that love and suffering are the same thing, the tall convict, unlike Harry, is finally unwilling to pay the price. Wilbourne and Charlotte welcome the passionate intensity which is a condition of their approach to life, even when it entails pain and sacrifice. It has got to be "either heaven, or hell," Charlotte tells Harry. "No comfortable safe peaceful purgatory between for you and me" (p. 83). The tall convict, on the other hand, opts for the safe peaceful purgatory; he willingly accepts the additional jail sentence because it means "ten more years to do without a woman" (p. 339). If the tall convict's return to Parchman is a retreat from the experience of living, it must not be forgotten, as Cleanth Brooks has pointed out, that he has proven that he can endure that experience.[14] In Faulkner's double novel there is an ideal operating throughout each of the contrapuntal stories. In "Wild Palms" Charlotte and Harry dedicate themselves to preserving in the twentieth century the same romantic ideal celebrated in medieval love lyrics. In "Old Man" the tall convict continually acts in accord with a moral ideal, which is not divorced from the chivalric pattern of behavior. "He wanted so little," the convict realizes of himself. "He just wanted to get rid of the woman, the belly, and he was trying to do that in the right way, not for himself, but for her. He could have put her back into another tree at any time—" (p. 161). In *The Wild Palms* Faulkner is writing of two men who are able to do more than either thought he could—not, as the tall convict says, for himself, but for the woman who caused all the grief.

In his discussions at Charlottesville Faulkner associates the battle against Snopesism (with "Snopes" representing to Faulkner a condition of exploitation in the twentieth century as much as the family of exploiters which symbolizes this condition—"a family," Montgomery Ward Snopes states in *The Mansion*, "a clan, a race, maybe even a species, of pure sons of bitches") specifically with the chivalric pattern of conduct. To the student who had just finished reading *The Town* and had seen Flem securely in possession of a house, a bank, a deacon's position in the Baptist church, and still going strong, and so who had asked if Snopesism would prevail in Jefferson, Faulkner's answer was no: "There is always someone that will never stop trying to cope with

[144]

Snopes, that will never stop trying to get rid of Snopes. . . .
The impulse to eradicate Snopes is in my opinion so strong
that it selects its champions when the crisis comes. When
the battle comes it always produces a Roland." While
Faulkner acknowledged that the Snopeses "are the men that
can cope with the new industrial age," the writer affirmed
that there will still be "something left of the old cavalier
spirit that will appear, that does appear. By cavalier spirit,
I mean people who believe in simple honor for the sake of
honor, and honesty for the sake of honesty" (*Faulkner in
the University*, pp. 34, 80). Faulkner's crusading Roland is
Gavin Stevens who like Quentin Compson tries to preserve
the chivalric code as an ideal of behavior in the twentieth
century and who unlike Quentin Compson "will never stop
trying" to make from this code viable principles of conduct.
To his nephew Chick Mallison, Gavin says in *Intruder in
the Dust*, "Some things you must always be unable to bear.
Some things you must never stop refusing to bear. Injustice
and outrage and dishonor and shame. . . . Not for kudos
and not for cash: your picture in the paper nor money in
the bank either. Just refuse to bear them" (p. 206).

Faulkner himself acknowledged that he saw in Don Quixote the prototype of Gavin Stevens, and he specifically
pointed to Gavin's fight with de Spain over Eula's honor
as a quixotic effort to defend somebody who does not want
to be defended and does not need it (*Faulkner in the University*, p. 141). Gavin together with the two other members
of the triumvirate—V. K. Ratliff, the sewing machine sales-
man whom Faulkner said he created and then fell in love
with, "a man who practiced virtue from simple instinct . . .
for a practical reason, because it was better" (*Faulkner in
the University*, p. 140), and Charles Mallison, who, as a
young boy in *Intruder in the Dust*, is brave enough to save,
almost single-handedly, Lucas Beauchamp from being

[145]

lynched—seek in *The Town* and *The Mansion* to fulfill their self-appointed task of protecting Jefferson from the onslaught of Snopeses. The degree of difficulty in such a task is evaluated by Ratliff: it is no more than checking a herd of tigers roaming loose all over the entire country. "No, we got them now; they're ourn now; I dont know jest what Jefferson could a committed back there whenever it was, to have won this punishment, gained this right, earned this privilege. But we did. So it's for us to cope, to resist; us to endure, and (if we can) survive" (*The Town*, p. 102). Of the three, however, it is Gavin who preserves in his behavior the chivalric ideal—particularly in his dedication to the protection of women, and generally in his quest to redress all wrongs not for reward but simply for virtue's sake. Gavin makes it his mission in *The Town* to give to Eula Varner Snopes the respectability she does quite well without. Either consciously or subconsciously he assigns to himself the role of cavalier by terming his defense of Eula's name a "crusade" (p. 49). Chick Mallison recognizes these chivalric principles behind his uncle's fight with de Spain at the Christmas cotillion—Gavin's protest against the mayor's dancing too close to Mrs. Snopes in "splendid unshame" (p. 75): "What he was doing was simply defending forever with his blood the principle that chastity and virtue in women shall be defended whether they exist or not" (p. 76). In addition to his role as defender of Eula's honor Gavin becomes the self-appointed protector of Linda Snopes against the threat of Snopesism. He buys her ice cream sodas, he makes suggestions about her reading, and in general busies himself with what his twin sister Maggie terms forming her mind (p. 187). But Gavin can also offer to pay for Linda's out-of-state school tuition in order to get her away from Jefferson—"Jefferson itself which was the mortal foe since Jefferson was Snopes" (p. 217). It is a protection which extends throughout the course of *The Town* and *The Mansion,* throughout Linda's tragic marriage to Barton Kohl, throughout her participation in Mink's murder of Flem, presumably up to that point when she gets in her new Jaguar and leaves Jefferson forever—and extends perhaps beyond.

In his class conferences at Charlottesville Faulkner himself commented on Gavin's shortcomings. He said that his county attorney knew the law very well. Where he got into trouble was in applying these legal tenets to the "real world in which people anguished and suffered, not simply did things which they shouldn't do" (*Faulkner in the University,* p. 140). Part of Gavin's trouble is his stubborn adherence to his imagination's construction of the world as it *should* be. Significantly it is the very same difficulty which confronted Cervantes' protagonist too—the impasse between a world in which action is prompted by ideal motives and a world in which action is prompted purely by practical considerations. That Gavin views the world in purely romantic terms is made clear by the scene in *The Town* in which he and Eula are discussing Flem's hold over Linda. Gavin has decided to tell Linda that she is illegitimate and so free her, he thinks, from Flem. Far from being a shock to her, Gavin imagines that the fact of her illegitimacy would be a source of pride, since it will make her one of "the world's immortal love-children": "Fruit of that brave virgin passion not just capable but doomed to count the earth itself well lost for love, which down all the long record of man the weak and impotent and terrified and sleepless that the rest of the human race calls its poets, have dreamed and anguished and exulted and amazed over—" (p. 226). His rhetoric is interrupted by the practical voice of Eula—who, in *The Town* is no longer mythicized to the degree she was in *The Hamlet* but is presented instead as a figure of capable intelligence:

[147]

"You dont know very much about women, do you?" she said. "Women aren't interested in poets' dreams. They are interested in facts" (p. 226).

In the same statement in which Faulkner discussed Gavin's shortcomings, he went on to make the interesting point that his love for abstract law, his passion for getting degrees was the part of his character which made him shy away from marriage. "He was probably afraid to be married," Faulkner continued. "He might get too involved with the human race if he married one of them" (*Faulkner in the University*, p. 141). When Eula visits Gavin's office and offers her body to him if he will drop his suit against her lover de Spain for stealing brass from the city powerhouse, Gavin's reaction is one of panic. As Eula moves toward him, having capably tended to the businesslike preparations of drawing down the shade, Gavin blocks her approach with his arm: " 'No, ' I said, cried. I might—would—have struck her with my out-flung arm, but there was room: out of the trap now and even around her until I could reach the door knob and open it" (p. 95). Gavin's motivation is complicated. Partly it is the reaction of the poet who is afraid to exist outside his dream, for fear reality might disappoint him. Partly it is the result of his mythologizing Eula—of seeing her as a Semiramis, a Helen, a Lilith, all in one. "You don't marry Semiramis," Maggie perceptively tells her brother (p. 50). She might have added that you just dedicate your whole life to serving her, to suffering and sacrificing for her in the service of love. Significantly Gavin does not marry Linda either, although both Eula and Ratliff ask it of him in order to save her finally from Flem. What Linda and Gavin have is an ideal Platonic relationship in which they can boast that they are "the two people in all the earth out of all the world" who do not need sex in order to achieve full love and trust in one another (*The Mansion*, p. 252). Their relationship is symbolically represented in *The Mansion* when they arrange to have adjoining rooms in the hotel. The wall between functions just as Tristan's sword does: it is a welcomed barrier to consummation. Although Faulkner's presentation of a panicked Gavin to Eula's Semiramis gently undercuts his role as a courtly lover, it does not negate the morally valid principles which lie behind his chivalric ideal. When Eula reprimands him for spending all his time in dreaming and in expecting, instead of simply taking what is offered him, Gavin is struck with the expediency of what she says: "If I had just had sense enough to say *I am, I want, I will and so here goes*—If I had just done that, it might have been me instead of Manfred. But dont you see? Cant you see? I wouldn't have been me then?" (p. 94). What Gavin is saying is that he must, by the very nature of his personality, act on his idealistic principles, not out of any hope for reward but for the sake of the principles themselves. Horace Benbow's answer to Ruby Goodwin's offering of herself in return for his legal defense of her accused husband in *Sanctuary* might be Gavin's answer too: "But cant you see that perhaps a man might do something just because he knew it was right, necessary to the harmony of things that it be done?" (p. 331). As Warren Beck points out, Gavin's idealistic conduct is in direct opposition to the concept of human relationships practiced as "mere barter," which is the limited view of life Eula has been exposed to;[15] and, as such, it merits her sincerest praise: "You're a gentleman," she tells Gavin, "and I never knew one before" (p. 94).

In terms of their chivalric pattern of conduct, Beck sees in Horace Benbow Gavin Stevens's prototype (*Man in Motion*, p. 110). Their biographies are strikingly similar. Both are county lawyers; both wed in their middle years. Like Gavin, Horace can cope perfectly well with the abstract theory of law. The particular affinity which he has for his

[149]

chosen vocation, Horace admits in *Sartoris*, is his "love for printed words"; his musty office is a source of pleasure because it is "the dwelling-place of books" (p. 175). Horace's glass blowing, the effete art which he brings back with him from the war, affords him hours of peace from the "real world in which people anguished and suffered," just as does Gavin's task of translating the Old Testament back into the classic Greek of its first translation. The extent to which Faulkner conceived of the two men as facets almost of the same personality is evidenced by the fact that in *Sartoris* he has Horace take Montgomery Ward Snopes with him to France to serve in the wartime YMCA; in *The Town* Gavin takes him. Both Gavin and Horace are dreamers. But while Gavin dreams in terms of chivalric images of crusade, Horace's dreams are pure escapism; while Gavin dreams of a world that ought to be, Horace dreams of a world that can never be. His imagination's construction is that of a fairy tale, "where unicorns filled the neighing air with galloping, or grazed or lay supine in golden-hoofed repose" (p. 179). And this is the important difference between the two men. When in *Sanctuary* Horace dares to confront evil, which is as much as part of the real world as goodness is, the experience proves too much for him. "You see, I lack courage," Horace tells Ruby Goodwin (p. 18). He retreats back into his imagination's world of fantasy—the "old unchanging days; unwinged perhaps, but undisastrous, too" (*Sartoris*, p. 175). He returns to his shrewish wife, Belle Mitchell, and in doing so we may assume he also returns to his Prufrockian task of bringing the dripping shrimp home to her at the appointed hour. After the Christmas cotillion when the chivalric tower which he has built around Eula collapses, Gavin goes to Heidelberg to seek refuge in still another degree. He does not leave, however, without first appointing Ratliff to be, in his absence, Jefferson's protector against

Snopesism (*The Town*, p. 102). More important Germany is not a permanent retreat for Gavin. Unlike Horace he dares to enter the fray once again when (in 1922) the vulnerability of the fourteen-year-old Linda calls out for a crusader.

Gavin's fight with Linda's beau Matt Levitt, after Matt has torn her dress in an amorous advance is, like his earlier fight with Manfred de Spain, an act of honor defended. In both instances Gavin's motivation is the same: it is the knight's "fevered projection of [his] mantle to defend and save her honor from its ravisher" (*The Town*, p. 91). And in both instances Gavin is equally unsuccessful—for all his cavalier intentions he is soundly bloodied by his antagonists. Chick's father chooses to see in his brother-in-law's gallantry an opportunity for some good-natured teasing. "What's the matter, boy?" he asks Gavin. "Where's your spear and sword? Where's your white horse?" (p. 185). While admitting that the quixotic gesture is comical, Faulkner himself also sees in it something a "little sad." He goes on to say too that "it is a very fine quality in human nature" and one which he hopes will always endure (*Faulkner in the University*, p. 141). After Gavin's fight at the Christmas cotillion, as accolade for his heroic act of gallantry Maggie gives a single red rose to her bleeding brother. Lying, she tells him it is from Eula. Because it is a lie, the rose becomes an ironic symbol of the love which Eula does not give in return. As one who neither wants to be defended nor needs to be, Eula is both unaware of and untouched by the chivalric act. For Faulkner, however, this ideal of conduct provokes his deepest admiration, as he himself has said, and thus there is more than a little truth behind Maggie's passionate cry: "You fool! You fool! They dont deserve you! They aren't good enough for you! None of them are, no matter how much they look and act like a—like a—like a god damn whorehouse! None of them! None of them!" (p. 77).

By virtue of his constant struggle with the forces of evil around him Gavin is one of Faulkner's "men in motion," and as such he is both the subject of Faulkner's writing and the object of his admiration. That Gavin, from a purely pragmatic point of view, is so rarely successful in his struggle is chiefly the result of the difficulty in applying his principles of love and honor and pity and pride and compassion and sacrifice to a practical world of private interest in which action is often prompted by material considerations. Nor is it only the Snopeses who, in Faulkner's Yoknapatawpha country, operate purely in terms of monetary gain. Even a character as admirable as Ratliff can be guilty of the same motive, when he is duped by Flem in the salting of the Old Frenchman's Place. The significance of Gavin's defeat, as John L. Longley, Jr., has pointed out, is that he prefers to be defeated by Snopesism rather than become a Snopes in order to win.[16] From an ethical point of view, the "defeat," then, paradoxically becomes a moral victory, which in the final analysis is the test by which all of Faulkner's characters are judged. Although confronted with setbacks, Gavin "will never stop trying"; as he himself says in *The Mansion* he will "just do the best he can" (p. 429), not out of any hope of reward but for simple virtue's sake. In the final book of the trilogy after Eula Snopes has taken her life, Gavin, bereaved, turns to Ratliff to help him understand the reason behind such an act. "Why did she do it, V. K.? That—all that—that she walked in, lived in, breathed in—it was only loaned to her; it wasn't hers to destroy and throw away. It belonged to too many. It belonged to all of us. Why, V. K.? . . . Why?" (p. 150). His poignant questioning reveals that until the very end Gavin remained true to his romantic construction of Eula as too much woman, too much glorious female for any one limited mortal to satisfy completely. At the same time the extent of his grief cannot be questioned;

if he created a goddess, he still reacted to her with the genuine passion and pain of the human heart. Having lost Eula, he loses Linda too, and judged in purely pragmatic terms, Gavin, because he receives no concrete compensation for "eighteen years of devotion," is once again defeated. "You haven't had very much, have you," Linda tells Gavin as she leaves Jefferson for the last time. "No, that's wrong. You haven't had anything. You have had nothing" (p. 424). Linda makes the mistake, however, of measuring Gavin against her terms of practical expediency and not by those idealistic principles which constitute *his* pattern of conduct. The point is that Gavin expected nothing in return. (There are "some things you must never stop refusing to bear," Gavin has said in *Intruder in the Dust:* "Injustice and outrage and dishonor and shame. . . . Not for kudos and not for cash. . . . Just refuse to bear them"). And it is not quite true either that he has not had anything. For him there is joy in the service itself. In answer to Linda, Gavin thinks back over the years of his devotion to her and to her mother and realizes that he had "got back for it nothing but the *privilege* of being obsessed, bewitched—" (*The Mansion*, pp. 424–25; italics mine). There is satisfaction, too, in living up to the high standards of his ideals—in knowing that he "just does the best he can." It remains for Ratliff to see in Gavin's "defeat" an ethical victory of those chivalric principles by which he lives: "Being the next-best to Paris is jest a next-best too, but it aint no bad next-best to be. Not ever body had Helen, but then not ever body lost her neither" (*The Town*, p. 101).

Few episodes in the Faulkner canon have aroused the degree of critical controversy as that provoked by the idyll of Ike Snopes and the cow in *The Hamlet*. John L. Longley sees it as a "high burlesque" of the situation and the language of courtly love. Irving Howe, Walter Slatoff, Richard P. Adams, and Walter Brylowski all concur that it is a parody of the romantic view of love as presented in the medieval romance. While never questioning the depth of their love, Olga Vickery states that "the element of humor in Ike's honeymoon with his seductive cow is unmistakable."[17] On its most literal level Faulkner is treating sodomy. Its human participant is an idiot, a fact to which Faulkner wishes to draw his reader's attention by the flashback describing at length Ike's earlier inability to descend Mrs. Littlejohn's stairs; he is presented, with more than a little pathos, as a bellowing figure of fear, clinging to the handrail at the top of the staircase, while a bemused audience gathers to watch from below. Howe and Slatoff, Adams and Brylowski are correct in seeing that behind the episode of Ike and the cow lie the conventions of the medieval romance. Ike Snopes successfully accomplishes—in spite of temptations to abandon it and difficulties to thwart it—his quest to save the object of his love from water, fire, and "dragon." Because of this heroic gesture the pathetic figure clinging to the top of the stairs is transformed into a contemporary protagonist of the knightly tales of valor; the object of Ike's love, Houston's cow, is similarly elevated and accordingly becomes the knight's lady—called Astarte, Juno, Troy's Helen. If Faulkner's tone in presenting the episode is comic, it is, however, genially so. If, while reading the story, we find ourselves laughing, we do not feel that we are laughing *at* Ike, and the laughter is tempered by pity not just for Ike, but for all less-than-omniscient devotees who ever gave themselves to less-than-perfect causes. While the element of humor is present, it does not, then, as many have maintained, undercut the chivalric mode and make a parody of the love idyll. Ike's capacity for devotion is never questioned, and his love is to be contrasted to the Snopeses' concept of human rela-

[154]

tionship as mere barter—the Snopeses, Ratliff said, who "established the foundations of their existences on the currency of coin" (*The Hamlet*, p. 202). It is significant that the scene immediately preceding the episode of Ike and the cow is that short passage which describes the illiterate Negro woman who comes straight from her chores in the fields to Will Varner's store and trades the new clerk, Lump Snopes, the pleasure of her body in exchange for a fifteen-cent can of sardines.

Faulkner partially sets apart the love idyll of Ike and the cow from the other sections of *The Hamlet* by his use of the highly rhetorical style peculiar to this episode. Warren Beck sees the lyric description of sunrise as an "artistically serviceable contrast to the perversion of the idiot Ike," while Mrs. Vickery perceives that the extravagant rhetoric points up the "excesses of the romantic view" presented.[18] The particular poetic quality of the language, however, seems to enforce rather than undercut the lofty tone of the medieval romance. T. Y. Greet recognizes in the style the richness of Spenser and suggests that this evocation has the effect of elevating the lovers into symbols.[19] It is true that Faulkner does not identify the two participants in the love drama until later in the section. The anonymous "he" and "she," placed against the framework of the chivalric romance, become simply lover and beloved enacting an idyll of love far removed from Frenchman's Bend and Yoknapatawpha County.

As in Quentin's re-creation of the Sutpen story as chivalric romance, the idyll takes place on the flower-filled May morning conventional to medieval love literature. Nature herself provides the ideal romantic backdrop for the lovers: "The trunks and the massy foliage were the harps and strings of afternoon" (p. 182). The particular description of the mist as drops of "the dawn's rosy miniatures" (p. 168) is a deliberate allusion to the description of "rosy-fingered dawn" in the aubade scene in *Romeo and Juliet,* and as such it evokes for comparison two of the world's most famous star-crossed lovers. As in the chivalric romance the object of the lover's veneration appears to be perfect in all attributes, both in comeliness of appearance and purity of soul. Seen through Ike's eyes his beloved is extolled as "blond" (only Shakespeare would allow the lady a dark complexion —and then only in jest!) and "dew-pearled"—with "bright thin horns of morning, of sun"(p. 168). To Ike the cow is "maiden meditant, shame-free" (p. 177). When in fear she loses control of her bodily functions, Ike treats the act as a medieval lover would the loss of his lady's virginity— "speaking to her, trying to tell her how this violent violation of her maiden's delicacy is no shame, since such is the very iron imperishable warp of the fabric of love" (p. 176). Because of her beauty of body and soul, Ike elevates his beloved into a goddess: "He watches himself contemplating what those who looked at Juno saw" (pp. 184–85). In the presence of such a superior being Ike exhibits the knight's humble adoration. As devoted swain he clumsily crowns her with a garland of daisies; as mooning courtly lover he daily makes his pilgrimage at dawn to the creek to await, for as long as three hours, the privilege of gazing at her. Their relationship is that ennobling passion which inspired the troubadours. To Ike the figure of the cow represents "the shape of love" (p. 169); the two, in Ike's mind, are "already married" (p. 167).

Ike willingly submits, as did Henry in Quentin's section of *Absalom, Absalom!,* to the reverential service which characterizes chivalrous youth of all times. Like Henry he dares to suffer and sacrifice for the sake of a love that is not easily attainable. In order to win the object of his love Ike must overcome the three obstacles that hinder his rescue of her

from a brush fire: first water, then fire, and finally the onslaught of Houston's horse, which to the mind of the idiot
assumes the monstrous shape of a fire-breathing dragon.
When Ike sees the smoke from the fire, his first concern
is for the safety of the cow. Although the omniscient author
points out that the fire was three miles away, Ike correctly
imagines his beloved is in danger—"he can even see her
backing away before the flames and hear her bellowing"
(p. 171). His first obstacle in the rescue is his ordeal in
crossing the creek to get to Houston's barn. Because he is
an idiot Ike does not even realize that he does not know how
to swim. He tries to run across the water as though it were
dry land, and when he plunges, in surprise and panic,
beneath the surface he gets up only to try again. He continues until he finally succeeds in crossing the creek, since that
creek is the barrier between himself and the voice of the
cow in distress, coming to him "faint and terrified" (p. 173).
The second obstacle is the brush fire itself, and although
Brylowski interprets the episode of Ike and the cow as a
parody of the knight's adventures in saving his lady he nevertheless points out the striking similarity of this particular
scene to the Siegfried myth with the circle of fire surround-
ing the maiden (*Faulkner's Olympian Laugh*, p. 145). Ike's
movements in fighting the fire are no less awkward than in
his attempt to cross the creek; he picks up first one foot,
then the other in a futile effort not to touch the scorching
ground, until soon "he was not progressing at all but merely
moving in one spot, like a dance." Like the water in the
creek, the fire represents to Ike the barrier "between him
and the location of the cow's voice," and as such he dares
to meet it headlong, heedless of his own safety: "Wild,
furious and without hope . . . he ran into and through the
fire . . . shedding flames which sucked away behind him
like a tattered garment." The third and last obstacle is

[157]

appropriately enough the attack by Houston's horse, which assumes, in Ike's terrified eyes, the frightening shape of a dragon and thereby becomes the archetypal foe in the fantastic tales of medieval romance. Faulkner forcefully renders Ike's terror as the horse, "monstrous and distorted," bears down on him: he screams in uncomprehending fright, until his bellowing finally merges with the horse's scream, until "his voice and that of the horse became one voice." Three times the horse charges at him, but Ike's love for the cow is finally stronger than his fear and he braves the monster—"the wild eyes, the yellow teeth, the long gullet red with ravening gleeful triumph . . . the fierce dragon-reek of its passage, blasting at his hair and garments" (p. 175).

Ike's chivalric attitude toward the cow is further emphasized by its deliberate contrast to Houston's treatment of her when he intrudes into their idyll. The broken willow branch with which Ike clumsily but gently washes the cow's flanks after she has fallen in the creek—an act of the courtly lover's devoted service—has as its counterpart the dried limb which Houston uses to "slash savagely" at the cow in an effort to get her out of the ravine, while at the same time shouting, "Git on home, you damned whore!" (p. 178). At this instant both Ike and Houston conceive of the cow as a woman; for Houston she is the cheap whore to Ike's courtly maiden. It is appropriate, then, that Houston should give the fifty-cent piece to Ike as reward for his rescuing the cow, for by doing so Houston makes the motive of this act monetary and thereby brings to the idyll once again his association of it with prostitution. When the coin falls into a ditch, it is fitting that Ike (described now by the author as peaceful and no longer bellowing) makes only one brief attempt to recover it—and "watching him you would have said he did not want to find the coin. And then you would have said, known, that he did not intend to find it" (p. 181).

In rejecting the coin Ike becomes one of the courtly lovers of all time to whom love is the only reward for the suffering and sacrifice performed in its service.

Having successfully overcome the knight's obstacles, Ike returns to claim his lady. With his quest completed and his reward enjoyed, Ike is elevated and becomes the prototype of the lover; his literal surroundings of the barnyard become transcendent, so that when Ike smells the odor of cows and mares it is "as the successful lover does that of a room full of women, his the victor's drowsing rapport with all anonymous faceless female flesh capable of love walking the female earth" (p. 183). By virtue of the shared act of love the cow is similarly elevated and becomes indistinguishable from the source of life. Her milk, flowing "among and about his fingers, hands, wrists," is identified with "the strong inexhaustible life ichor itself, inherently, of itself, renewing." Together the two lovers become archetypes—"original, in the womb-dimension, the unavoidable first and the inescapable last, eyeless." By virtue of the ennobling quality of their love, Ike and the cow have transcended the chivalric and attained the more heroic, timeless dimension of myth, and so when Ike drinks at the spring it becomes "the well of days, the still and insatiable aperture of earth. It holds in tranquil paradox of suspended precipitation dawn, noon, and sunset; yesterday, today, and tomorrow" (p. 188). It is interesting to note that the description of the bower where Ike and the cow lie—the terrestrial canopy over the slumbering "Helen and the bishops, the kings and the graceless seraphim" (p. 189)—echoes almost verbatim the passage in *The Mansion* in which Mink, having accomplished his mission by killing Flem, is assimilated into the ground. Because they have successfully completed the quest, performed the heroic act, both Ike and Mink have earned the privilege of being judged in such exalted company.

Ike's idyll is brought abruptly to an end at that moment when the plank is pulled off the barn and admission is charged. It is appropriate that the Reverend Whitfield's "cure" should fail because he treats only the sodomous aspect of the affair (kill the cow and beef it, he instructs; then have him eat it, knowing who it is, and he will turn to *human* females), while he ignores the fact of love. Six months after the cow is killed, Ratliff sees Ike in the empty stall with the battered wooden effigy of a cow, and because it *was* love, he sees "the blasted face," "the devastated eyes" (p. 271). It is significant too that the Snopes who profanes the love by selling space for all Yoknapatawpha to watch it is Launcelot ("Lump") Snopes, named so because his mother believed "that there was honor and pride and salvation and hope too to be found for man's example between the pages of books" (p. 200). Because Lump makes a travesty of that chivalric principle which lies behind his name, he is one of the many examples in Faulkner in which the perversion of the principle points by implication to the positive case—to a Gavin Stevens or Quentin Compson "who believe in simple honor for the sake of honor, and honesty for the sake of honesty" —or to Ike Snopes who is brave enough to act on that principle although he is unable to articulate it, or even to understand it.

# CHAPTER V

# The Heroic Ideal

In his fictional world of Yoknapatawpha County—a community essentially of yeomen and small tenant farmers—Faulkner is writing of people who are searching, both consciously and unconsciously, for a heroic ideal. The very nature of the search is for success of such a kind as to make failure inevitable as Richard P. Adams points out in *Faulkner: Myth and Motion* (p. 221, n. 15). That complete victory is finally unattainable has led some critics to assert that Faulkner is commenting on the negative qualities in human nature, or, at best, on the inability of the individual, however well-intentioned or admirable he may be, to cope with the circumstances which confront him.[1] Walter J. Slatoff has inverted the existing situation in his *Quest for Failure*. André Malraux sees in Faulkner's work "an inexorable, even epic force" whenever "he succeeds in bringing one of his characters up against the irremediable"; and he concludes that "perhaps the irremediable is his only true subject, perhaps his only aim is to crush man."[2] Faulkner himself has said that he refuses to accept the end of man—that man will not merely endure but will prevail. To those who do not see this degree of affirmation running consistently throughout Faulkner's works, his statement is countered by the argument that after receiving the Nobel prize the writer felt a greater sense of his responsibility as a public figure and accordingly a need to affirm in his later works those positive values he had expounded in his speech at Stockholm.[3] Edith Hamilton denies even this change in Faulkner's novels after 1950. She sees in the Nobel prize acceptance speech "that singular swing to elevation" which Schopenhauer noted in great literature, but states that it is totally absent in Faulkner's writings: "In his books he reminds us only of the futility of all things human, and the certain defeat of all men's struggles."[4] And yet in a letter to Warren Beck, written in 1941, Faulkner indicates that his original intention all along had been to glorify the human condition: "I have been writing all the time about honor, truth, pity, consideration, the capacity to endure well grief and misfortune and injustice and then endure again, in terms of individuals who observed and adhered to them not for reward but for virtue's own sake. . . . I believe there are some, not necessarily many, who do and will continue to read Faulkner and say, 'Yes. It's all right. I'd rather be Ratliff than Flem Snopes. And I'd still rather be Ratliff without any Snopes to measure by even.' "[5]

When asked at Nagano if he considered human life basically a tragedy, Faulkner answered in the affirmative, but then went on to say it was to man's credit that when faced with a tragedy which he cannot overcome he still tries to do something with it: "Man strives for the eternal verities of the human heart—courage, pride, honor, compassion. He wants to be better than he is afraid that he might be—that he might fail, yet he still tries." It is this act of trying, Faulkner adds, that is the source of man's immortality.[6] It is what makes Byron Bunch so admirable at that moment when he sees the figure of the fleeing Lucas and decides to pursue it for the simple, selfless motive that this is what Lena wants: "I took care of his woman for him and I borned his child for him. And now there is one more thing I can do for him. I cant marry them, because I aint a minister. And

I may not can catch him, because he's got a start on me. And I may not can whip him if I do, because he is bigger than me. But I can try it. I can try to do it" (*Light in August*, p. 373).

Conversely the individual who merits Faulkner's censure is the one who is unwilling to enter the fray, whose attitude is represented by the young Jewish pilot in *A Fable* who says, "This is terrible. I refuse to accept it, even if I must refuse life to do so." Horace Benbow is an example of one who must be included in this group. When faced in *Sanctuary* with the purgative experience of evil, he is finally unable to cope with it, and he retreats once again into his world of glass blowing and unicorn-filled daydreams—the "old unchanging days; unwinged perhaps, but undisastrous, too" (*Sartoris*, p. 175). Rosa Coldfield is another, and the room in which she shuts herself for forty-three years, brooding over the memory of Thomas Sutpen's insult and writing Civil War odes which reflect no first-hand knowledge of the brutality of war, becomes, in its "coffin-smelling gloom," the tomb which appropriately symbolizes Rosa's separation from the world of reality. Isaac McCaslin too must be numbered in this group. After relinquishing the McCaslin plantation, he chooses to live out his life alone in the woods in a vain effort to recapture some part of his lost original innocence. In this retreat he proves himself finally unequal to the heroic pageant he had once been allowed to witness, and he is justifiably rebuked by the granddaughter of Tennie's Jim as being indirectly responsible for Roth's actions in "Delta Autumn." It is significant that the gesture which saves Gail Hightower and which prevents him from being included with the Horace Benbows and Rosa Coldfields is his delivery of Lena Grove's baby, an act which literally is a direct involvement with life.

Although Faulkner subjects his characters to situations of

great stress, his aim is not, as Malraux contends, "to crush
man" but rather to test him, to show just how much he is
capable of enduring—and one is tempted to agree with
Heinrich Straumann when he says that endurance is "the
one single highest value that Faulkner does not question by
a contrast to its own category."[7] The act of endurance
involves, of course, great strength. It also involves great
suffering, but Faulkner's characters are ennobled by their
suffering where the characters of, say, Eugene O'Neill are
not. "God dont tell you to suffer," Nancy Mannigoe says
in *Requiem for a Nun*, "but He gives you the chance"
(p. 278). In *The Wild Palms* Charlotte equates love and
suffering and in doing so espouses what is really the chivalric
code without its artificiality: "The second time I ever saw
you," she tells Harry, "I learned what I had read in books
but I never had actually believed: that love and suffering are
the same thing and that the value of love is the sum of what
you have to pay for it." And again, in exacting from her
husband the promise not to prosecute Harry if she should
die from the abortion, she says: "For your sake maybe, since
yours is suffering too—if there is any such thing as suffering,
if any of us ever did, if any of us were ever born strong
enough and good enough to be worthy to love or suffer
either" (pp. 48, 225–26). So often in Faulkner the degree
of admiration which we feel for a given character is in direct
proportion to what that character is made to undergo—
Cash Bundren, for example, or Judith Sutpen, who loses a
fiancé whom she loves very much and a brother she loves
equally as well, and after the loss is willing to care for that
fiancé's son by another woman. It is an act which involves
compassion and selflessness—and a great deal of pain. There
is a feeling too that the catharsis which comes at the moment Joe Christmas is dying and which brings him the
peace he had fruitlessly pursued is earned as a kind of recom-

pense for the violent death he is made to suffer and for the life lived in terrible loneliness, symbolized by the street without end which he "was to run for thirty years." It is perhaps easy to overlook how much the tall convict goes through because his story is told in a comic mode, but he is presented as a Job figure who, together with the woman in the tree, suffers "all the crises emotional social economic and even moral which do not always occur even in the ordinary fifty married years" (*The Wild Palms,* p. 254). It is significant too that those commentators who deny Thomas Sutpen full heroic stature do so because he fails to undergo the tragic hero's moment of self-recognition and with it the anguish attendant on such a discovery. Thus Shreve wonders how Sutpen could *"be allowed to die without having to admit that he was wrong and suffer and regret it"* (p. 305).

Like the old Greeks Faulkner believed in a moral universe, in the dualistic existence of good and evil; and it is this belief that precludes any kind of final and complete victory in his works. As the Reverend Sutterfield says in *A Fable,* "evil is a part of man, evil and sin and cowardice, the same as repentance and being brave. You got to believe in all of them, or believe in none of them. Believe that man is capable of all of them, or he aint capable of none" (p. 203). Snopesism, as Faulkner has indicated, is a perennial condition in human nature, and as such it will persist long after the individual members of the Snopes clan have destroyed one another. But the impulse to eradicate Snopesism is also a condition of human nature, and when the inevitable battle between the two comes, Faulkner says, it will always produce a Roland: "There's always someone that will never stop trying to cope with Snopes, that will never stop trying to get rid of Snopes. . . . It doesn't mean that they will get rid of Snopes or the impulse which produces Snopes, but

[165]

always there's something in man that don't like Snopes and objects to Snopes and if necessary will step in to keep Snopes from doing some irreparable harm" (*Faulkner in the University*, p. 34). The universal battle against Snopesism is, as Faulkner views it, a continuing ordeal; as has been discussed earlier, it is expressed in terms of the chivalric mode of conduct, and in both of these respects the struggle itself calls to mind Spenser's quest of the Red Cross Knight—it is the good fight you fight all of your life.

"There are good men everywhere, at all times," Isaac McCaslin says in "Delta Autumn." "Most men are. Some are just unlucky, because most men are a little better than their circumstances give them a chance to be. And I've known some that even the circumstances couldn't stop" (*Go Down, Moses*, p. 345). In a 1955 interview Faulkner was asked about the instances in his novels when his characters are defeated, and to the question he gave a most interesting answer: there is always in his work one person who survives, he said, who triumphs over his fate[8]—or, as Ike would say, whom even the circumstances could not stop. Faulkner himself pronounced V. K. Ratliff capable of coping with change because he possessed a "moral, spiritual eupepsia"—"a man who practiced virtue from simple instinct . . . for a practical reason, because it was better" (*Faulkner in the University*, pp. 253, 140). When the Snopes tribe invades Frenchman's Bend in the trilogy, V. K. does not hesitate to take up the gauntlet: "No, we got them now; they're ourn now. . . . So it's for us to cope, to resist; us to endure, and (if we can) survive" (*The Town*, p. 102). Judith Sutpen is another who meets, with dignity, the circumstances which confront her—and Dilsey, who when faced with the Compsons' problems of alcoholism, suicide, promiscuity, and idiocy, somehow manages to hold the family together and to give to them the love of which they

[166]

themselves are incapable. There are also Charles Mallison and Miss Habersham, a young boy and an old woman, who together persevere against dangers, both physical and metaphysical, until they succeed in saving Lucas Beauchamp from being lynched. Young Bayard is yet another who is capable of performing the heroic act. In his refusal to avenge his father's death he earns not only Faulkner's praise and Aunt Jenny's—but Drusilla's too. The tall convict suffers all manner of trials known to man and endures them only to suffer again—until his mission is complete: "Yonder's your boat, and here's the woman," he says to the deputy at Parchman. "But I never did find that bastard on the cottonhouse" (*The Wild Palms*, p. 278). In his total devotion to Lena Grove, Byron Bunch is a most admirable character; and although in the course of the novel he does not succeed in his personal quest, there is every reason to believe that in time he will do so: "I done come too far now," Byron tells Lena. "I be dog if I'm going to quit now." And Lena, looking back at him, "hangdog and determined and calm too, like he had done desperated himself up for the last time": "Aint nobody never said for you to quit" (*Light in August*, p. 443).

In a comment at Charlottesville Faulkner restated the purpose of his writing: "It's man in the ageless, eternal struggles which we inherit and we go through as though they'd never happened before, shown for a moment in a dramatic instant of the furious motion of being alive" (*Faulkner in the University*, p. 239). By juxtaposing these struggles against the framework of classical drama or epic or the chivalric romance, Faulkner is suggesting that the prototypes of his characters are to be found in ancient Greek literature or in medieval poetry. These particular genres have this in common—that they presuppose the significance of man. "A

[167]

tragic writer does not have to believe in God," Joseph Wood Krutch states, "but he must believe in man." Though the action of tragedy is nearly always calamitous, Krutch goes on to say, there is nevertheless affirmation even in this aspect—since "it is only in calamity that the human spirit has the opportunity to reveal itself triumphant over the outward universe which fails to conquer it."[9] Edith Hamilton proclaims Homer to be the spokesman of the Greeks and says that in his two epics lies "the conviction that gods were like men and men able to be godlike." Sounding curiously like Faulkner she defines this godlike quality to be "the courage and undaunted spirit with which the heroes faced any opponent, human or divine, even Fate herself."[10] In the chivalric code, as practiced by Cervantes' Don, is the glorification of man's "softer virtues"—love as devoted service, honor, loyalty to the concepts of courtesy, valor, and generosity. In his juxtaposition of Yoknapatawpha with this framework of allusion, Faulkner is signifying that his rural community is to be measured against a set of older heroic ideals with the implication that people can still be as diabolical as Faust or perhaps even Satan himself, as crusading as Roland, as beautiful as Helen, as devoted as Tristan, as brave as Odysseus. It is this comparison which I believe Faulkner had in mind when he expressed his reason for preferring the Old Testament over the New: "The New Testament is full of ideas and I don't know much about ideas. The Old Testament is full of people, perfectly ordinary normal heroes and blackguards . . . trying to be braver than they are." They were people "doing the best they could"—and then he added, "just like people do now" (*Faulkner in the University*, pp. 167, 286).

Many commentators have detected in *The Mansion* a resurgence of Faulkner's earlier imaginative powers, specifically in his treatment of the Mink Snopes material. It involves the solitary quest of an old man who has nothing in his favor but his own indomitable will, who persists against all manner of obstacles and hardships until he completes his self-appointed mission to kill his cousin Flem. At that point when he succeeds in accomplishing the gesture Faulkner's illiterate sharecropper is accordingly elevated and becomes one with the old heroes of myth and legend: "equal to any, good as any, brave as any, being inextricable from, anonymous with all of them: the beautiful, the splendid, the proud and the brave." Mink Snopes is as near an archetype of the perennial underdog as any character to be found in Faulkner. Gavin Stevens says that Mink is "a little kinless tieless frail alien animal that never really belonged to the human race to start with, let alone belonged in it." "The sort of a creature whom nobody, even his victim, noticed enough in time to pay any attention to what he was or might do" (*The Mansion*, pp. 392–93, 381). Economically and socially he belongs to the class of the southern poor white; he lives in a paintless two-room cabin, for which he pays "almost as much in rent in one year as the house had cost to build." This extreme poverty which is Mink's existence is apparently his destiny too, for his cabin is "just like the one he had been born in which had not belonged to his father either, and just like the one he would die in if he died indoors" (*The Hamlet*, p. 223).

In his creation of Mink it is as though Faulkner reduced his character as far as it would go and still deserve to be called man and then stood back to see if there were anything in what remained that would stand forth and declare its humanity. And indeed perhaps this is the source of one's admiration of Mink—that knowing that there is nothing outside himself which will in any way help him to get through the ordeal of living, make that ordeal any less difficult, he must rely totally on himself as the sole defender of his own simple rights as a member of the human race; and so all his moments become "connected, involved in some crisis of the constant outrage and injustice he was always having to drop everything to cope with, handle, with no proper tools and equipment for it, not even the time to spare from the unremitting work it took to feed himself and his family" (*The Mansion,* p. 405). Nor are Mink's actions, however primitive they may be, without principle; it is an attribute which makes him unique among his family clan— "the only Snopes," Cleanth Brooks says, "with a sense of honor" (*The Yoknapatawpha Country,* p. 221). When he is caught in the ruse of trying to winter his cow on the property of a farmer more prosperous than he, Mink endures the backbreaking labor of paying Houston back at the rate of fifty cents per day, just as he endures Houston's forbidding him to work his land at night—an act which puts an end to his attempt to furrow his own farm by day and thereby care for his family: "He could stand that too. Because he knew the trick of it. He had learned that the hard way; himself taught that to himself through simple necessity: that a man can bear anything by simply and calmly refusing to accept it, be reconciled to it, give up to it" (p. 21). The obligation itself, however, is a duty which Mink will not shirk, and thus he refuses Houston's offer to pay him *pro gratis* for three days' work so he can go home and plant his own crop, just as he refuses Will Varner's attempt to buy back the cow. What finally outrages Mink is the extra one-dollar pound fee which Houston charges; it is an affront to his own pride in himself as a man, and as such one can imagine Mink feeling what Gavin Stevens is able to articulate: "Some things you must always be unable to bear. Some things you must never stop refusing to bear. Injustice and outrage and dishonor and shame" (*Intruder in the Dust,* p. 206). The fee is the final insult which Mink refuses to tolerate; it is the reason that he shoots Houston, as he himself makes known to the dying man (p. 39). To Mink the murder is justified. He imagines the shot itself as defying "that conspiracy to frustrate and outrage his rights as a man and his feelings as a sentient creature" (*The Hamlet*, p. 222).

Mink's motivation in killing Flem is the same that prompted him to shoot Houston—both are presented as an act of honor vindicated. When Mink is on trial for the murder of Houston, he pays no attention to any of the legal proceedings going on in the courtroom but instead keeps his eyes fastened on the door waiting confidently for Flem to come, as clan loyalty dictates, and use his influence to free him of the charges. It is a conviction held by more than just Mink; and so Bookwright continues to insist to Ratliff that Flem will help his cousin: "Aint no man, I dont care if his name is Snopes, going to let his own blood kin rot in jail" (*The Hamlet*, p. 325). Not only does Flem not come, but, anticipating his cousin's desire for revenge after he is released from Parchman, he arranges with Montgomery Ward Snopes for Mink's abortive escape attempt. In the attempt Mink proves himself worthy of admiration. Having realized he has again been tricked by his kin, Mink chooses to run right at the deputies—"to run right at his fate"—and watching him, Montgomery Ward thinks to himself: "I was proud, not just to be kin to him but of belonging to what Reba called all of us poor son of a bitches. Because it took five of them striking and slashing at his head with pistol barrels and even then it finally took the blackjack to stop him, knock him out." This outrage which adds twenty years to his jail sentence is compounded by the shame involved in the particular disguise which Flem has persuaded him to wear—"a petticoat and a woman's sunbonnet"; "a man should be permitted to run at his fate," Mink says, "in the decency and dignity of pants." This shame corresponds to

Houston's extra pound fee; it is the final insult which Mink will not brook: "I reckon you'll see Flem before I will now," he tells Montgomery. "Tell him he hadn't ought to used that dress. But it dont matter. If I had made it out then, maybe I would a changed. But I reckon I wont now. I reckon I'll jest wait" (pp. 85–86).

Wait Mink does—all told, thirty-eight years—for the opportunity to kill Flem and thereby earn "the right to have his own just and equal licks back" (p. 6). Cleanth Brooks sees in Mink's single-minded purpose "something literally out of this world—certainly out of the world of the twentieth century." His desire for revenge, Brooks concludes, "is almost as selfless and detached as that of a character in an Elizabethan revenge play" (*The Yoknapatawpha Country*, p. 232). In this quest, just as in every ordeal Mink has ever had to confront, he has no outside help of any kind, nothing going for him except an unshaking belief in "a simple fundamental justice" which he calls "Old Moster." "Old Moster jest punishes," he says with conviction over and over again, "He dont play jokes" (p. 407). As the belief in this conviction grows, Mink himself seems to become an instrument of the same sense of justice which he commends: *If a feller jest wants to do something, he might make it and he might not. But if he's GOT to do something, cant nothing stop him*" (p. 49). As in his effort to settle his account with Houston, Mink's conduct continues to be based on principle. However badly he needs money to buy a gun and ammunition to kill Flem, he will still refuse the two hundred and fifty dollars Gavin had arranged with the warden to give to him if he will only promise to leave Mississippi. Nor will he steal, even if he has every right to do so. When the ten dollars he has earned in helping Goodyhay build his church is stolen, he realizes he has a thousand times more need to steal in return but he does not: *"No. I aint never stole. I aint*

*never come to that and I wont never"* (p. 274). In the face
of these setbacks Mink perseveres in his purpose, "asking
no favors of any man, paying his own way" (p. 8). He persists
until with the "snub-nosed, short-barrelled" pistol, rusted
over and resembling the relic of some antediluvian terrapin
(p. 291), with the one precious bullet that remains to him,
he succeeds in killing Flem. The act itself is more nearly
heroic than Mink's earlier slaying of Houston; this time the
murder is no ambush.

There is a decided change in Mink after he accomplishes
his quest. In *The Town* V. K. had called him "the only
out-and-out mean Snopes we ever experienced" (p. 79); and
throughout the trilogy he is constantly referred to in terms
of animal imagery—"no more pitiable than a scorpion"
(*The Mansion*, p. 287); "a different kind of Snopes like a
cotton-mouth is a different kind of snake" (*The Hamlet*,
p. 92); "a worn-out dried-up shrimp of a man" (*The Mansion*, p. 83)—and, as in the case of Popeye, the imagery
implies a being less than human. But after the murder of
Flem—and thereby because of the magnitude of what he,
unaided, has been able to do—the old Mink Snopes is puri-
fied. After he shoots Flem, Mink walks westward; it is the
direction of a free man. He is even willing now to put aside
his lifelong fear of the land—"the ground, the dirt which
any and every tenant farmer and sharecropper knew to be
his sworn foe and mortal enemy—the hard implacable land
which wore out his youth and his tools and then his body
itself" (p. 90). Like Joe Christmas Mink has earned his
peace, and unafraid he lies on the earth itself. Almost at
once he starts to feel "the Mink Snopes that had had to
spend so much of his life just having unnecessary bother and
trouble, beginning to creep, seep, flow easy as sleeping"
(p. 435). He is lulled back further than simply to his own
innocent beginnings. It is a journey backward to the old

heroic past, and Mink becomes one with all mortals and deities who too once pursued an ideal: "Helen and the bishops, the kings and the unhomed angels, the scornful and graceless seraphim" (p. 436).

It is perhaps fitting that *The Reivers*, Faulkner's last work, should call forth scenes and situations from his earlier novels. The setting is the same as in *Sanctuary*—Miss Reba's brothel. But here she is young, and as Michael Millgate points out, "the world, though sinning lustily, is somehow more innocent than it later became."[11] The perilous journey from Jefferson to Memphis to Parsham, Tennessee, evokes the Bundren odyssey in *As I Lay Dying*, with the ordeal in trying to cross the muddy swamp of Hell Creek bottom having a particular parallel in the Bundrens' efforts to maneuver their team across the flooded river. But here the nature of the journey is not nearly so somber as in the earlier novel. It has nothing at all to do with death but instead is undertaken for the most frivolous of motives, as three kinghts-errant, enjoying that degree of freedom known only when supervision is suddenly—and only temporarily—removed, set off in pursuit of the promise of high adventures. The theme of the novel is the same that Faulkner treated at great length in "The Bear"—the initiation of a young boy into manhood. There is even a character link with Faulkner's earlier story. The bumbling, good-natured Boon Hogganbeck, smitten with Miss Corrie and so convincing Lucius to steal the family automobile so he can get to Memphis to see her, is the same Boon Hogganbeck who kills old Ben. Lucius Priest, from whose vantage point the story is told, is a distant kin of old Lucius Quintus Carothers McCaslin, and it is his name that he bears. Ned McCaslin, who of the three most loves an adventure—so much so that he is thoroughly willing to stir one up where none is to be found—boasts a more direct descent from the male line; thus he will not let Lucius's family forget that he "was an actual grandson to the old time-honored Lancaster where we moiling Edmondses and Priests . . . were mere diminishing connections and hangers-on" (*The Reivers*, p. 31). Finally, as in "The Bear," Faulkner juxtaposes young Lucius's loss of innocence against mythic allusions to the Fall of man, but it is with this difference—that the presentation is entirely comic in spirit and not tragic.[12]

The opportunity for adventure presents itself when Lucius's mother, father, and grandfather are called out of town to attend a funeral. With Boon in possession of the car keys the temptation proves too great, and the two, with Ned as stowaway, set out to Memphis, to the big city. Structurally *The Reivers* is a retrospective narrative; and the engagingly happy tone of the novel is, in part, owing to this fact. The Yoknapatawpha County of 1905, remembered fifty-six years later, called forth from Lucius's childhood, takes on (as Cleanth Brooks points out) "something of the attraction of a country in romance: there were giants in those days and there were worthy giant killers" (*The Yoknapatawpha Country*, p. 351). Indeed the particular obstacles which confront the three on the road to Memphis have more than a little in common with the trials found in storybook tales of the long ago and far away. The first, the mudhole of Hurricane Creek, is a physical challenge which Boon is able to meet when, by virtue of pure brute strength, he lifts the automobile from up off the ground and hurtles it forward to dry land. The second, the Iron Bridge, is directly identified with the archetypal foe in fairy tales and romance, since it is associated with "an ancestryless giant calling himself Ballenbaugh" (p. 73). The third and by far the greatest test of their ingenuity is the trial at Hell Creek bottom, where the "primeval setting of ooze and slime and jungle growth

[175]

and heat" is pitted against the automobile, their age's symbol of progress—and discovered, to their dismay, to be no contest at all.

Hell Creek bottom, or the last obstacle which stands between Boon, Ned, and Lucius and Memphis, their destination, is described in terms of mythic and historical associations, all of which have to do with the motif of the journey—a journey which, in this case, represents Lucius's passage from innocence to experience. Hell Creek is compared to Lethe (p. 92), the river in mythology from which the souls of the dead must drink before they are allowed to enter again the cycles of birth and death. Significantly in "The Fire and the Hearth" Lucas Beauchamp imagines himself also crossing "a kind of Lethe" at that moment when Zack Edmonds, because he is white, orders Molly, because she is black, into his house to care for his newborn son and to satisfy his own physical needs. This is Lucas's rebirth into the world of experience: "It was as though on that louring and driving day he had crossed and then recrossed a kind of Lethe, emerging, being permitted to escape, buying as the price of life a world outwardly the same yet subtly and irrevocably altered" (*Go Down, Moses*, p. 46). The obstacles themselves—the only barriers between Jefferson, or the familiar world of his childhood, and Memphis—are compared by Lucius to the Rubicon; the comparison implies a point of no return which, once passed, ensures his own spiritual journey into manhood: "Because the die was indeed cast now; we looked not back to remorse or regret or might-have-been; if we crossed Rubicon when we crossed the Iron Bridge into another county, when we conquered Hell Creek we locked the portcullis and set the bridge on fire" (p. 93). Walter Brylowski makes an interesting and valid point when he calls the old woodsman who plows up the creek to create a sea of mud and then charges exorbitant prices for the loan of his mules to get travelers across a Charon figure.[13] This comparison together with the particular name of the swamp, Hell Creek, evokes the soul's crossing the River Styx on its passage to the underworld; it specifically anticipates Lucius's experience in Memphis of what he calls "non-virtue"—and in particular his visit to Miss Reba's brothel.

Olga Vickery contends that once Lucius crosses his Rubicon, he leaves behind the real world of ordinary event and commonplace happening, which is Jefferson, for a world in which the laws of nature are suspended and replaced by "the fabulous and the magical" (*Novels*, p. 231). Although events on the other side of the locked portcullis do verge at times on the fantastic, what Lucius discovers in Memphis and later in Parsham is the world of good and evil of which Faulkner has all along been writing. Lucius himself will call it "non-virtue" and, with his grandfather's help, will in time finally come to accept the world as such: since evil exists, one must "learn about it, know about it; hating that such not only was, but must be, had to be if living was to continue and mankind be a part of it" (p. 174). *The Reivers* is basically an apprenticeship novel, and this discovery of the existence of nonvirtue is the essence of Lucius's newfound knowledge. His initiation is significantly juxtaposed against the story of another who also pursued enlightenment. When Lucius first leaves Jefferson, he does so in a mood of joyful anticipation. Boon has acknowledged him to be the smarter of the two, and with the compliment Lucius "feels suddenly that same exultant fever-flash which Faustus himself must have experienced: that of we two doomed and irrevocable, I was the leader, I was the boss, the master" (p. 53). But after the four-day sojourn in which he encounters much more than any eleven-year-old boy bargained for, Lucius experiences the disillusionment which is also a part of growing up: he realizes "the true shoddy worthlessness of the soul [he] had been vain enough to assume the devil would pay anything for" (p. 58). With the realization Lucius becomes a very unwilling Faust figure, with no desire at all now "to probe the hidden": "I knew too much, had seen too much. I was a child no longer now; innocence and childhood were forever lost, forever gone from me" (p. 175). Feeling a sense of guilt from "all the lying and deceiving and disobeying and conniving" he had done and a great deal of homesickness, Lucius has more than a little in common with the protagonist of "The Bear." Like Isaac McCaslin he yearns for his own lost innocence; and so Lucius must resist the desire to "return, relinquish, be secure" (p. 66).

But *The Reivers* is a comic novel, and the forces of evil which Boon and Ned and Lucius encounter in Memphis and Parsham are soundly defeated by the forces of good. Perhaps it is because of his innocence and idealism that Lucius conceives of the world in chivalric terms. From the moment he first meets Miss Corrie in Reba's brothel he makes it his task to protect her good name, and in this respect he has a great deal in common with another of Faulkner's crusaders—Gavin Stevens. Lucius repeatedly defends Corrie against the amorous advances of both Boon and Butch Lovemaiden, the "stallion deputy sheriff" whose courtly name belies his intentions. The action evokes Gavin's fights with de Spain at the Christmas cotillion and later with Matt Levitt; in each instance the motivation is the same: it is the knight's projection of his "mantle to defend and save [his lady's] honor from its ravisher" (*The Town*, p. 91). But there is a sense that for all his eleven years Lucius is a real protection to Corrie where Gavin, of course, is not to Eula. And so Uncle Parsham Hood, the old Negro patriarch, says to Ned: "He's stood everything else you folks got him into since you brought him here. . . . Didn't he have to watch it too . . . that man horsing and studding at that gal, and her trying to get away from him, and not nobody but this eleven-year-old boy to run to? not Boon Hogganbeck and not the Law and not the grown white folks to count on and hope for, but just him?" (p. 225).

When the horrible little Otis tells him that Corrie is a prostitute, Lucius fights for her honor, and like Gavin he is bloodied in the attempt—his hand is cut by Otis's open knife. Unlike Eula, however, Corrie responds to the gallantry of the act: "You fought because of me," she tells Lucius. "I've had people—drunks—fighting over me, but you're the first one ever fought for me." The act is what prompts her to give up prostitution. "I want to make you a promise," she says to her young protector. "Back there in Arkansas it was my fault. But it wont be my fault any more." Her promise becomes an oath, and she makes Lucius say aloud that he accepts it as such (pp. 159–60). Corrie's decision to reform is not without its humorous aspects, coming at that moment just when Boon has made the long trip to Memphis to see her. But the point is that Lucius's defense of her honor is no quixotic gesture as was Gavin's. She lives up to Lucius's ideal of her, a transformation evidenced when she chooses to drop the name given to her by the madam, and to take, in its stead, her own again—Everbe Corinthia, with its connotation of purity and chastity, which Lucius has all along called her. Nor is the young boy's chivalric gesture lost on Boon, who, in comparison, is totally lacking in terms of a gentlemanly code of conduct. When Corrie breaks her oath on that one occasion in order to ensure the return of Lightning in time to run the race, he is not above blackening her eye. But when Butch makes insulting remarks about the woman he loves, Boon fights her antagonist and in doing so repeats Lucius's courtly behavior: "God damn it . . . if you can go bare-handed against a knife

[179]

defending her, why the hell cant I marry her? Aint I as good as you are, even if I aint eleven years old?" (p. 299).

As befits the comic novel, *The Reivers* can boast of the conventional happy ending. Lucius succeeds in transforming the prostitute into an honest woman, and Boon makes of her a wife. Once Mr. Poleymus, the constable at Parsham, has "walked up to Butch and snatched that pistol outen his hand and reached up and ripped that [deputy-sheriff's] badge and half his shirt off too," the villain of the piece gets his just deserts. Nor does Miss Reba's servant Minnie go unrewarded, for in the course of the novel she recovers her precious gold tooth. As for Ned, he manages to win his race, knowing the secret of the sardine-loving race horse. Though Ned's scheme seems fantastic—"to use the horse to win the automobile back from the man that has already give [him] the horse for it" (p. 119)—there are, nevertheless, high stakes in the balance. A victory will do no less than enable Ned and Lucius and Boon to return safely again home. As Lucius says, "if the successful outcome of the race this afternoon wasn't really the pivot; if Lightning and I were not the last desperate barrier between Boon and Ned and Grandfather's anger, even if not his police . . . then all of us were engaged in a make-believe not too different from a boys' game of cops and robbers" (pp. 229–30).

Of *The Reivers* Olga Vickery says that "it is a tribute to Faulkner that in this, his last book, he should have created his world by describing man not tragically, satirically, or comically but simply lovingly" (*Novels*, p. 239). The particularly warm and happy tone of the novel is not, as some have maintained, evidence of a late mellowing on Faulkner's part. Rather it is a difference not of kind but perhaps of degree from what had gone before. If Faulkner writes of the anguishes of man and the baseness of which he is capable, he writes too of his aspirations and courage—"the splendor of man, of the human heart" (*Faulkner in the University*, p. 103). If he writes tragedy which always stops history, as in the story of Thomas Sutpen or Joe Christmas, he also writes comedy in which life goes on. In that statement in which he said he would most like to have written *Moby-Dick* because of "the Greek-like simplicity of it," Faulkner also gave an alternate choice which is equally revealing: "And yet, when I remember Moll Flanders and all her teeming and rich fecundity like a market-place where all that had survived up to that time must bide and pass . . . I can wish without any effort at all that I had thought of that."[14] The statement suggests a polarity in Faulkner's thinking which is also evident in his writings. Often he will balance a tragic mode with an essentially comic approach to life: the Compson disintegration with the Bundren odyssey, in which all except Darl return safely home; Charlotte's death with the tall convict's successful rescue of the woman in the tree; the story of Joe Christmas with Lena Grove's perseverance in her journey—"a fur piece." In each case the last glimpse the reader has is of the character who continues on, still participating in "the furious motion of being alive." This idea of continuation is itself an affirmation. It is what Faulkner has been saying all along, in his letter to Warren Beck, at Nagano, at Charlottesville, at Stockholm: "Man is tough . . . nothing, nothing—war, grief, hopelessness—can last as long as man himself can last . . . man himself will prevail over all his anguishes, provided he will make the effort to."[15] At the University of Virginia Faulkner explicitly stated that his basic conception of life was optimistic. That conception indicates that in regard to the human condition he himself was above despair, believing, like Isaac McCaslin, that "most men are a little better than their circumstances give them a chance to be."

[181]

# Notes

## CHAPTER I

1. *Faulkner in the University,* ed. Frederick L. Gwynn and Joseph L. Blotner (New York: Vintage Books, 1965), p. 199.

2. "Myth and Literary Classicism," in *The Modern Tradition: Backgrounds of Modern Literature,* ed. Richard Ellmann and Charles Feidelson, Jr. (New York: Oxford University Press, 1965), p. 681.

3. In discussing *Old Man* at Charlottesville, Faulkner said that the humor in the tale did not undercut what had been performed—successfully. It was just a tool, he said, to tell the comic and the tragic conditions of man in coping with himself, his fellow man, and his environment (*Faulkner in the University,* p. 177). That the character of the tall convict commanded Faulkner's fullest admiration is also revealed by the writer: "The river's whole purpose [in *Old Man*] had been . . . to give man another chance to prove, not to him but to man, just how much the human body could bear, stand, endure." Faulkner goes on to add that it "would have made a weaker or a less centered man blench and falter, but not him." See "Mississippi," *Holiday,* April 1954, rpt. in James B. Meriwether, ed., *Essays, Speeches and Public Letters by William Faulkner* (New York: Random House, 1965), pp. 25–26; *Faulkner in the University,* p. 176.

4. Vincent Hopper recognizes the epic proportions of Faulkner's works, but he concludes that the writer's world is finally unredeemed and damned—an Inferno "with no Paradise in view." In his analysis Hopper sees in Faulkner only the baseness of which the individual is capable; his novels become the chroni-

cle, Hopper says, of the "impotence, ignorance, and bewilderment
. . . of the twentieth-century man." See "Faulkner's Paradise
Lost," *Virginia Quarterly Review*, 23 (Summer 1947), 405–20.
Faulkner himself said that he was writing not just about the
troubles and anguishes of man, but also about his aspirations and
courage—"the splendor of man, of the human heart" as well as
the baseness (*Faulkner in the University*, p. 103).

5. Frederick J. Hoffman and Olga W. Vickery, eds. (New York:
Harbinger Books, 1963), pp. 28–29.

## CHAPTER II

1. Walter Sullivan, "The Tragic Design of *Absalom, Absalom!*," *South Atlantic Quarterly*, 50 (October 1951), 560.

2. Aristotle, *Poetics*, trans. Ingram Bywater, in *Introduction to Aristotle*, ed. Richard McKeon (New York: Random House, 1947), p. 640.

3. *William Faulkner: The Yoknapatawpha Country* (New Haven, Conn.: Yale University Press, 1963), p. 313. Hereafter referred to in the text as *The Yoknapatawpha Country.*

4. Andreas Capellanus makes frequent mention of the Paradise and Purgatory of lovers in his writing. Similarly, in *The Sound and the Fury*, Quentin desires an eternal union with Caddy in that "clean flame" of Hell: "If it could just be a hell beyond that: the clean flame the two of us more than dead. Then you will have only me then only me" (p. 135).

5. "Ancient Myths and the Moral Framework of Faulkner's *Absalom, Absalom!*," *American Literature*, 35 (May 1963), 200. Throughout I have used the King James Version of the Bible (New York: Oxford Univ. Press, n.d.).

6. "The Historical Novel and the Southern Past: The Case of *Absalom, Absalom!*," *Southern Literary Journal*, 2 (Spring 1970), 75–76.

7. *Faulkner in the University*, p. 35. The following recognize in *Absalom, Absalom!* the elements of classical tragedy: Melvin Backman, "Sutpen and the South: A Study of *Absalom, Absalom!*," *PMLA*, 80 (December 1965), 596–604; Lennart Björk, "Ancient

Myths and the Moral Framework of Faulkner's *Absalom, Absalom!*," 196–204; Brooks, *William Faulkner: The Yoknapatawpha Country;* C. Hugh Holman, *Three Modes of Modern Southern Fiction: Ellen Glascow, William Faulkner, Thomas Wolfe* (Athens: University of Georgia Press, 1966); Vincent Hopper, "Faulkner's Paradise Lost," 405–20; Ilse Dusoir Lind, "The Design and Meaning of *Absalom, Absalom!*," *PMLA*, 70 (December 1955), 887–912; John L. Longley, Jr., *The Tragic Mask: A Study of Faulkner's Heroes* (Chapel Hill: University of North Carolina Press, 1963). Longley names Sutpen as one of Faulkner's tragic heroes, but sees Colonel John Sartoris as the character in Faulkner who "most clearly fulfills all the criteria of the traditional classic hero" (p. 178); Michael Millgate, *The Achievement of William Faulkner* (New York: Random House, 1966); George Marion O'Donnell, "Faulkner's Mythology," *Kenyon Review*, 1 (Summer 1939), 285–99; Walter Sullivan, "The Tragic Design of *Absalom, Absalom!*," 552–66; Olga Vickery, *The Novels of William Faulkner*, 2nd ed., rev. (Baton Rouge: Louisiana State University Press, 1964).

8. Letter to the book editor, *Chicago Tribune*, 16 July 1927, rpt. in James B. Meriwether, ed., *Essays, Speeches and Public Letters by William Faulkner*, pp. 197–98.

9. In classical tragedy the concept of the tragic flaw combines two discordant elements—nobility and proneness to error—without reconciling them. "It thus suggests the element of paradox which seems essential to the greatest tragedy." See the *Princeton Encyclopedia of Poetry and Poetics*, ed. Alex Preminger (Princeton: Princeton University Press, 1965), p. 864.

10. "Faulkner's Tragedy of Isolation," in *Southern Renascence: The Literature of the Modern South*, ed. Louis D. Rubin, Jr., and Robert D. Jacobs (Baltimore: Johns Hopkins Press, 1966), p. 186. Jacobs ultimately views Sutpen not as a Greek hero, but as a Renaissance hero.

11. The following statements are based on Quentin and Shreve's piecing together of the Sutpen story, a version which rests on the supposition that Bon was Sutpen's son by a part-Negro wife. For

the existence of real evidence to support this point—and the plausibility of Quentin and Shreve's version in general—see Cleanth Brooks's discussion of *Absalom, Absalom!* in *The Yoknapatawpha Country*, pp. 314–17. Brooks states that Quentin received his information from a most reliable witness—from the dying Henry Sutpen on the occasion of Quentin's and Miss Rosa's visit to Sutpen's Hundred.

12. *Absalom, Absalom!* is not without elements of humor. See for instance Shreve's perspective of the Sutpen story; Rosa's outraged reaction to Thomas Sutpen, notably in the wild chariot race to church; the scene in which the French architect desperately tries to escape from Sutpen and his band of wild Negroes by using his suspenders to catapult himself from tree to tree. More than any other of Faulkner's works, however, *Absalom* is by far the most serious in tone and conception. Aristotle points out the rigorous distinction on the Attic stage between tragedy and comedy, with comedy clearly considered to be the inferior mode. J.A.K. Thomson, in *The Classical Background of English Literature* (1948; rpt. New York: Collier Books, 1962, p. 33) observes that Milton approved of this distinction and condemned "the error of intermixing comic stuff with tragic sadness and gravity, or introducing trivial or vulgar persons."

13. "The Design and Meaning of *Absalom, Absalom!*," *PMLA*, 70 (December 1955), rpt. in *Three Decades of Criticism*, p. 290.

14. *Classical Influences on English Poetry* (1951; rpt. New York: Collier Books, 1962), p. 105.

15. In accounting for the special elevation of the prose style in *Absalom, Absalom!* Walter Sullivan observes that "the language of the [ordinary] novel is unable to sustain the emotional and intellectual intensity that is inherent in much dramatic poetry" ("The Tragic Design of *Absalom, Absalom!*," p. 553).

16. "Sutpen and the South: A Study of *Absalom, Absalom!*," *PMLA*, 80 (December 1965), 603.

17. Sutpen's failure to gain insight into his fault is justified by

the very framework of Greek tragedy itself. A heroic character "may arrive sooner or later at a recognition of his place in the universe, of a relationship between his character and his fate, or he may apprehend less about his experience than do other characters . . . or the audience, thus creating situations of tragic irony." (*Princeton Encyclopedia of Poetry and Poetics*, pp. 860–61). That Sutpen never realizes his sin is not to say, however, that the discovery scene integral to Greek tragedy is missing in *Absalom, Absalom!* It comes at that moment when Sutpen recognizes the identity of Judith's suitor; and as in classical tragedy it is closely linked to hamartia. Sutpen's discovery of the truth of the matter is his full and ghastly wakening from that state of ignorance which was the very essence of his tragic error.

18. "The Tragic Fallacy," *The Modern Temper* (1929; rpt. New York: Harcourt, 1956), p. 86.

19. Lennart Björk sees Agamemnon as the most consistently used image of comparison with Sutpen, and he says that the action of Faulkner's protagonist should be viewed against Agamemnon's sacrificing his daughter—and ultimately his wife—in order to forward his design of conquering Troy ("Ancient Myths and the Moral Framework of Faulkner's *Absalom, Absalom!,*" pp. 197–98).

20. Sophocles, *Oedipus the King,* trans. Theodore H. Banks, in *Three Theban Plays* (New York: Oxford University Press, 1956), 11. 783–84. Subsequent references are to this edition and are parenthetically placed in the text.

21. Sophocles, *Antigone,* trans. Theodore H. Banks, in *Three Theban Plays,* 1. 529. Subsequent references are to this edition and appear in the text.

22. "Faulkner's Mythology," *Kenyon Review,* 1 (Summer 1939), rpt. in *Three Decades of Criticism,* p. 86.

## CHAPTER III

1. Ike's love idyll with the cow, presented in terms of the framework of the chivalric romance, will be discussed at length in chapter four.

2. *The Achievement of William Faulkner* (New York: Random House, 1966), p. 194.

3. *The Power of Blackness* (New York: Knopf, 1967), p. 108.

4. "The Biblical Rhythm of *Go Down, Moses*," *Mississippi Quarterly*, 20 (Summer 1967), 138. Mellard also sees the biblical myth of Eden and the Fall as unifying the narrative, theme, and characters in *Go Down, Moses*. This analogue is not fully developed, however, especially as it applies to "The Bear," by far the most important story in *Go Down, Moses*.

5. Milton, as Faulkner seems to do, associates fertility with the divine process of Creation. In *Paradise Lost* Adam's roses in the garland he has made for Eve wither when he sees that she has fallen. It is the first entry of death into Paradise.

6. *The American Adam: Innocence, Tragedy, and Tradition in the Nineteenth Century* (Chicago: University of Chicago Press, 1955), p. 5.

7. See Olga Vickery's discussion of "The Bear" in *The Novels of William Faulkner*, 2nd ed., rev. (Baton Rouge: Louisiana State University Press, 1964), pp. 131–34. Hereafter referred to in the text as *Novels*.

8. These biblical passages which support Isaac's decision to repudiate the McCaslin plantation are cited by Francis Lee Utley in his "Pride and Humility: The Cultural Roots of Isaac McCaslin," in *Bear, Man, and God: Seven Approaches to William Faulkner's The Bear*, ed. Utley et al. (New York: Random House, 1964), p. 249.

9. "The Irony of Southern History," in *Southern Renascence*, p. 66.

10. *The Yoknapatawpha Country*, p. 268. Andrew Lytle's discussion is to be found in "Faulkner's *A Fable*," *Sewanee Review*, 63 (Winter 1955), 127–28.

11. *Faulkner's Olympian Laugh: Myth in the Novels* (Detroit: Wayne State University Press, 1968), p. 164.

12. *Faulkner: Myth and Motion* (Princeton: Princeton University Press, 1968), pp. 144–45.

13. Henry James, Sr., quoted in *The American Adam*, p. 55.

14. *Faulkner at Nagano,* ed. Robert A. Jelliffe (Tokyo: Kenkyu-sha, 1956), pp. 77–78. In "Delta Autumn" the granddaughter of Tennie's Jim reprimands Ike for spoiling Roth by giving land to Roth's grandfather which did not belong to him "by will or law" (p. 360). The accusation implies that Isaac in relinquishing the McCaslin plantation to Cass in "The Bear" was indirectly responsible for Roth's actions in "Delta Autumn."

15. *Faulkner in the University,* p. 2. Walter Brylowski (in *Faulkner's Olympian Laugh,* p. 158) calls the snake harmless and identifies it not as the snake of Eden but as yet another incorporation of the spirit of the wilderness.

16. Carvel Collins perceives that the gum tree is located at the dividing line between "civilization" and the primitive forest, but he does not see this in terms of an Adamic framework. See "A Note on the Conclusion of 'The Bear,'" *Faulkner Studies,* 2 (Winter 1954), 59.

17. "Faulkner's Tragedy of Isolation," in *Southern Renascence,* p. 254.

18. *"As I Lay Dying* as Ironic Quest," *Wisconsin Studies in Contemporary Literature,* 3 (Winter 1962), 5–19.

19. London: Macmillan, 1908, p. 22.

20. See Barbara Cross, "Apocalypse and Comedy in *As I Lay Dying," Texas Studies in Literature and Language,* 3 (Summer 1961), 251–58. Miss Cross discusses Faulkner's use of apocalyptic imagery in the novel, but like Elizabeth Kerr she concludes that the selfish motives which some of the Bundrens have for reaching Jefferson finally serve to make "a parody of myth" (p. 258).

21. *The Achievement of William Faulkner,* p. 110. When asked if the "very highly suggestive" names of his characters were coincidental or intentional, Faulkner replied that the latter was the case: "That is out of the tradition of the pre-Elizabethans, who named their characters according to what they looked like or what they did. . . . Of course, it seems to me that those people named themselves, but I can see where that came from—it came from the—my memory of the old miracle plays, the morality plays in early English literature" (*Faulkner in the University,* p. 97).

22. Richard P. Adams (in *Faulkner: Myth and Motion*, p. 75) says that the river symbolizes a "profound transformational experience, a rebirth involving a change of identity and a shifting of all individual relations to the world and time." Adams is correct in seeing the symbolic connotation of the river, but the point is that the evoked baptism does not occur.

23. Interview with Jean Stein, *Paris Review*, 4 (Spring 1956), rpt. in *Three Decades of Criticism*, p. 73. Cf. *Faulkner in the University*, p. 87. Richard Adams in *Faulkner: Myth and Motion* also sees *As I Lay Dying* as patterned after the epic journey, but he does not discuss in detail the specific ways in which Faulkner uses the analogue.

24. See Cross, "Apocalypse and Comedy in *As I Lay Dying*," p. 256.

25. Interview with Jean Stein, p. 81.

26. *Form and Fable in American Fiction* (New York: Oxford University Press, 1965), p. 81.

27. From the 1925 Oxford University Press translation by Sir William Marris. See Carvel Collins, "The Pairing of *The Sound and the Fury* and *As I Lay Dying*," *Princeton University Library Chronicle*, 18 (Spring 1957), 123. Collins also cites the eleventh book of the *Odyssey* (Marris translation) as the possible source for Faulkner's title.

## CHAPTER IV

1. Quoted in *Faulkner at West Point*, ed. Joseph L. Fant III and Robert Ashley (New York: Random House, 1964), p. 54.

2. "Faulkner: The South, the Negro, and Time," in *Faulkner: A Collection of Critical Essays*, ed. Warren (Englewood Cliffs, N.J.: Prentice-Hall, 1966), p. 269.

3. "Life on the Mississippi," *The Writings of Mark Twain* (New York: Harper, 1904), IX, 347.

4. New York: Vintage Books, 1941, pp. 46–47.

5. New York: Braziller, 1961, p. 45.

6. *The Burden of Southern History* (Baton Rouge: Louisiana State University Press, 1960), p. 345.

7. Olga Vickery (in *The Novels of William Faulkner*, p. 79) interprets the vision to mean that Hightower is retreating into the past again. The vision, she suggests, affords an escape from the bitter self-knowledge which the minister has the intelligence to attain but lacks the strength to live with. Because this matter of Hightower's final vision is ambiguous, it will perhaps be advantageous to look closely at how Faulkner presents it. The chapter opens several hours after Christmas's murder, with the old minister again at his window, waiting as in the past for the vision of his grandfather on horseback. Hightower is thinking back over his life, focusing especially on the events of failure. The thinking itself is compared to the movement of a wheel, here presented as a medieval instrument of torture which torments not his body but his mind and spirit. The wheel's movement is geared to Hightower's agonized thoughts, proportionately grinding slower and slower as Hightower draws nearer to some kind of revelation: "Thinking is running too heavily now; he should know it, sense it. Still the vehicle is unaware of what it is approaching" (p. 429). The anticipated moment of truth comes with Hightower's acknowledgment that he has failed both his wife and his congregation because of his obsession with his grandfather's memory. At this instant the wheel suddenly releases its pressure, thus suggesting resolution: "The wheel, released, seems to rush on with a long sighing sound. He sits motionless in its aftermath. . . . The wheel whirls on. It is going fast and smooth now, because it is freed now of burden, of vehicle, axle, all" (p. 430). It is at this point that Hightower experiences his vision, and the tone is triumphant: "It is as though they [the Confederate ghosts] had merely waited until he could find something to pant with, to be reaffirmed in triumph and desire with, with this last left of honor and pride and life" (p. 431). Whether or not Hightower dies as he hears the "dying thunder of hooves" is really beside the point. Though the knowledge comes very late, the minister does succeed, as Cleanth Brooks has said, in "fathoming his nature"—in seeing himself as he really is and in accepting the responsibility: "Whether Hightower died or lived on, he had broken out of the circle in which we find him

at the opening of the story" (*The Yoknapatawpha Country*, p. 71).

8. Southern chivalry in general focused on the idealization of woman so emphatically, W. J. Cash points out in *The Mind of the South*, that it could be termed "downright gyneolatry" (p. 89).

9. *Love in the Western World* (1939; rpt. New York: Anchor Books, 1957), p. 45.

10. Interview with Jean Stein, p. 75.

11. "The Tradition of Romantic Love and *The Wild Palms*," *Mississippi Quarterly*, 25 (Summer 1972), 274.

12. *Quest for Failure: A Study of William Faulkner* (Ithaca, N.Y.: Cornell University Press, 1960), p. 207.

13. See, for example, Joseph J. Moldenhauer, "Unity of Theme and Structure in *The Wild Palms*," in *Three Decades of Criticism*, pp. 305–22; Hyatt H. Waggoner, *William Faulkner: From Jefferson to the World* (Lexington: University of Kentucky Press, 1959), pp. 132–45; Vickery, *The Novels of William Faulkner*, pp. 156–66.

14. "The Tradition of Romantic Love and *The Wild Palms*," p. 281.

15. *Man in Motion: Faulkner's Trilogy* (Madison: University of Wisconsin Press, 1963), p. 110. While acknowledging Gavin's difficulty in coping with the world around him, Beck has high praise for his chivalric code of conduct: he is "the protagonist of the ethic which is most explicit in putting women and children first but which applies in defense of all common human rights. . . . Gavin's quixotism is not an aberration but simply an extravagance . . . and if it is cavalier, it is gallantly so, sensing honor vitally as something . . . to be lived up to in progressive conduct" (p. 136).

16. *The Tragic Mask: A Study of Faulkner's Heroes* (Chapel Hill: University of North Carolina Press, 1963), p. 49.

17. Longley, *The Tragic Mask*, p. 224; Howe, *William Faulkner: A Critical Study* (New York: Vintage Books, 1952), p. 85; Slatoff, *Quest for Failure*, p. 94; Adams, *Myth and Motion*, p. 117; Brylowski, *Faulkner's Olympian Laugh*, p. 145; Vickery, *The Novels of William Faulkner*, p. 178.

18. Beck, "William Faulkner's Style," *American Prefaces*, 6

(Spring 1941), rpt. in *Three Decades of Criticism*, pp. 143–44; Vickery, *The Novels of William Faulkner*, p. 179.

19. "The Theme and Structure of Faulkner's *The Hamlet*," *PMLA*, 72 (September 1957), rpt. in *Three Decades of Criticism*, p. 340. Greet is one of the few commentators who sees the episode of Ike and the cow as a serious evocation of the medieval romance.

## CHAPTER V

1. See, for example, Malcolm Cowley, Introduction, *The Portable Faulkner* (New York: Viking, 1946), p. 16.

2. Preface to *Sanctuary* (Paris, 1949), pp. 7–8.

3. See Irving Howe, *William Faulkner: A Critical Study*, pp. 289–90; James B. Meriwether, ed., *Essays, Speeches and Public Letters by William Faulkner*, p. viii; William Van O'Connor, *William Faulkner*, University of Minnesota Pamphlets on American Writers, No. 3 (Minneapolis: University of Minnesota Press, 1959), p. 39; Hyatt H. Waggoner, *William Faulkner: From Jefferson to the World*, p. 213.

4. "William Faulkner," *The Ever-Present Past* (New York: Norton, 1964), pp. 170–71.

5. Cited in Beck, "Faulkner: A Preface and a Letter," *Yale Review*, 52 (October 1962), 159.

6. *Faulkner at Nagano*, p. 4; and cf. *Faulkner at West Point*, p. 76.

7. "An American Interpretation of Existence: Faulkner's *A Fable*," *Anglia*, 73 (1955), rpt. in *Three Decades of Criticism*, p. 371.

8. Interview with Cynthia Grenier, *Accent*, 16 (Summer 1956), 172.

9. "The Tragic Fallacy." *The Modern Temper*, pp. 87, 84.

10. *The Greek Way* (1943; rpt. New York: Norton Library, 1964), p. 177.

11. *The Achievement of William Faulkner*, p. 253.

12. For a discussion of Faulkner's presentation of Lucius's loss of innocence in the metaphor of the fall, see Brylowski, *Faulkner's Olympian Laugh*, pp. 215 and following.

13. *Faulkner's Olympian Laugh*, p. 217.

14. Letter to the book editor, *Chicago Tribune*, 16 July 1927, rpt. in Meriwether, ed., *Essays, Speeches and Public Letters by William Faulkner*, p. 198.

15. "To the Youth of Japan," in *Faulkner at Nagano*, p. 186.

# Index